P9-EGL-835

CliffsNotes™

Lord of the Flies

By Maureen Kelly

IN THIS BOOK

- Learn about the Life and Background of the Author
- Preview an Introduction to the Novel
- Study a graphical Character Map
- Explore themes and literary devices in the Critical Commentaries
- Examine in-depth Character Analyses
- Reinforce what you learn with CliffsNotes Review
- Find additional information to further your study in CliffsNotes Resource Center and online at www.cliffsnotes.com

Wiley Publishing, Inc.

About the Author
Maureen Kelly is a freelance writer and editor and a Master's candidate at DePaul University.

Publisher's Acknowledgments

Editorial
Project Editor: Tracy Barr
Acquisitions Editor: Greg Tubach
Glossary Editors: The editors and staff of Webster's New World Dictionaries
Editorial Assistant: Michelle Hacker

Composition
Indexer: York Production Services, Inc.
Proofreader: York Production Services, Inc.

Wiley Indianapolis Composition Services

CliffsNotes™ *Lord of the Flies*

Published by:
Wiley Publishing, Inc.
111 River Street
Hoboken, NJ 07030
www.wiley.com

Copyright © 2000 Wiley Publishing, Inc., New York, New York
ISBN: 0-7645-8597-5
Printed in the United States of America
15 14 13 12
1O/SU/QY/QR/IN
Published by Wiley Publishing, Inc., New York, NY
Published simultaneously in Canada

Library of Congress Cataloging-in-Publication Data
Kelly, Maureen, 1969-
   CliffsNotes Lord of the Flies / by Maureen Kelly.
      p. cm.
   Includes biographical references and index.
   ISBN 0-7645-8597-5 (alk. paper)
   1. Golding, William, 1911- Lord of the Flies--Examinations--Study guides. 2. Survival after airplane accidents shipwrecks, etc., in literature. I. Title: Lord of the Flies. II. Title.

PR6013.O35 L634 2000
823'.914--dc21   00-036946
                                                       CIP

No part of this publication may be reproduced, stored in a retrieval system, or transmitted in any form or by any means, electronic, mechanical, photocopying, recording, scanning, or otherwise, except as permitted under Sections 107 or 108 of the 1976 United States Copyright Act, without either the prior written permission of the Publisher, or authorization through payment of the appropriate per-copy fee to the Copyright Clearance Center, 222 Rosewood Drive, Danvers, MA 01923, 978-750-8400, fax 978-646-8600. Requests to the Publisher for permission should be addressed to the Legal Department, Wiley Publishing, Inc., 10475 Crosspoint Blvd., Indianapolis, IN 46256, 317-572-3447, fax 317-572-4447, or e-mail permcoordinator@wiley.com

For general information on our other products and services or to obtain technical support, please contact our Customer Care Department within the U.S. at 800-762-2974, outside the U.S. at 317-572-3993, or fax 317-572-4002.

Wiley also publishes its books in a variety of electronic formats. Some content that appears in print may not be available in electronic books.

Table of Contents

How to Use This Book

This CliffsNotes study guide on William Gerald Golding's *Lord of the Flies* supplements the original literary work, giving you background information about the author, an introduction to the work, a graphical character map, critical commentaries, expanded glossaries, and a comprehensive index, all for you to use as an educational tool that will allow you to better understand *Lord of the Flies*. This study guide was written with the assumption that you have read Lord of the Flies. Reading a literary work doesn't mean that you immediately grasp the major themes and devices used by the author; this study guide will help supplement your reading to be sure you get all you can from Golding's *Lord of the Flies*. CliffsNotes Review tests your comprehension of the original text and reinforces learning with questions and answers, practice projects, and more. For further information on William Gerald Golding and *Lord of the Flies*, check out the CliffsNotes Resource Center.

CliffsNotes provides the following icons to highlight essential elements of particular interest:

Reveals the underlying themes in the work.

Helps you to more easily relate to or discover the depth of a character.

Uncovers elements such as setting, atmosphere, mystery, passion, violence, irony, symbolism, tragedy, foreshadowing, and satire.

Enables you to appreciate the nuances of words and phrases.

Don't Miss Our Web Site

Discover classic literature as well as modern-day treasures by visiting the Cliffs-Notes Web site at www.cliffsnotes.com. You can obtain a quick download of a CliffsNotes title, purchase a title in print form, browse our catalog, or view online samples.

You'll also find interactive tools that are fun and informative, links to interesting Web sites, tips, articles, and additional resources to help you, not only for literature, but for test prep, finance, careers, computers, and the Internet too. See you at www.cliffsnotes.com!

LIFE AND BACKGROUND OF THE AUTHOR

The following abbreviated biography of William Gerald Golding is provided so that you might become more familiar with his life and the historical times that possibly influenced his writing. Read this Life and Background of the Author section and recall it when reading Golding's *Lord of the Flies*, thinking of any thematic relationship between Golding's work and his life.

Personal Background

William Gerald Golding was born in Cornwall, England, in 1911. His mother, Mildred, was a strong supporter of the British suffragette movement. His father, Alec, was a schoolteacher and an ardent advocate of rationalism, the idea that reason rather than experience is a necessary and reliable means through which to gain knowledge and understand the world. Alec's anti-religious devotion to reason was the legacy of such scientific rationalists as T.H. Huxley and H.G. Wells. This rationalist viewpoint was not tolerant of emotionally based experiences, such as the fear of the dark that Golding had as a child. His father wielded a tremendous influence over him, and, in fact, until leaving for college, Golding attended the school where his father taught.

Education

Golding began attending Brasenose College at Oxford in 1930 and spent two years studying science, in deference to his father's beliefs. In his third year, however, he switched to the literature program, following his true interests. Although his ultimate medium was fiction, from an early age, Golding dreamed of writing poetry. He began reading Tennyson at age seven and steeped himself in Shakespeare's work. While still at Oxford, a volume of Golding's poems was published as part of Macmillan's Contemporary Poets series. Later in life, Golding dismissed this work as juvenile, but these poems are valuable in that they illustrate his increasing distrust of the rationalism he had been reared on, mocking well-known rationalists and their ideas. In 1935, he graduated from Oxford with a Bachelor of Arts in English and a diploma in education.

Jobs

From 1935 to 1939, Golding worked as a writer, actor, and producer with a small theater in an unfashionable part of London, paying his bills with a job as a social worker. He considered the theater his strongest literary influence, citing Greek tragedians and Shakespeare, rather than other novelists, as his primary influences.

In 1939, Golding began teaching English and philosophy in Salisbury at Bishop Wordsworth's School. That same year, he married Ann Brookfield, with whom he had two children. With the exception of five years he spent in the Royal Navy during World War II, he remained in the teaching position until 1961 when he left Bishop Wordsworth's School to write full time.

Golding died in Cornwall in 1993.

Literary Writing

The five years Golding spent in the navy (from 1940 to 1945) made an enormous impact, exposing him to the incredible cruelty and barbarity of which humankind is capable. Writing about his wartime experiences later, he asserted that "man produces evil, as a bee produces honey." Long before, while in college, he had lost faith in the rationalism of his father with its attendant belief in the perfectibility of humankind. While Golding's body of fiction utilizes a variety of storytelling techniques, the content frequently comes back to the problem of evil, the conflict between reason's civilizing influence, and mankind's innate desire for domination.

Novels

In *Lord of the Flies*, which was published in 1954, Golding combined that perception of humanity with his years of experience with schoolboys. Although not the first novel he wrote, *Lord of the Flies* was the first to be published after having been rejected by 21 publishers. An examination of the duality of savagery and civilization in humanity, Golding uses a pristine tropical island as a protected environment in which a group of marooned British schoolboys act out their worst impulses. The boys loyal to the ways of civilization face persecution by the boys indulging in their innate aggression. As such, the novel illustrates the failure of the rationalism espoused by Golding's father.

A fast, intense writer, Golding quickly followed *Lord of the Flies* with *The Inheritors* (1955), a depiction of how the violent, deceitful *Homo sapiens* achieved victory over the gentler Neanderthals. Although this novel is the one readers have the most difficulty understanding, it remained Golding's favorite throughout his life.

Pincher Martin followed in 1956. Like *Lord of the Flies*, it concerns survival after shipwreck. Navy lieutenant Christopher Martin is thrown from his ship during combat in World War II. He finds a rock to cling to, and the rest of the story is related from this vantage point, detailing his struggle for survival and recounting the details of his life.

Golding uses the flashback technique of *Pincher Martin* more extensively in his next novel, *Free Fall* (1959). Unlike his first three novels, *Free Fall* is told with a first person narrator, an artist named Samuel Mountjoy. The novel takes as a model Dante's *La Vita Nuova*, a collection of love poems interspersed with Dante's own commentary on the poems. Golding uses the character Mountjoy to comment on the conflict between rationalism and faith.

Issues of faith are addressed in *The Spire* (1964) as well. A fourteenth-century Dean of Barchester Cathedral decides that God wants a 400-foot-high spire added to the top of the cathedral, although the cathedral's foundation is not sufficient to hold the weight of the spire. The novel tells the story of the human costs of the spire's construction and the lessons that the Dean learns too late.

The Pyramid (1967) provides an examination of English social class within the context of a town ironically named Stilbourne. A primary issue in this story is music, and the novel utilizes the same structure as the musical form sonata.

Golding's next publication was a collection entitled *The Scorpion God: Three Short Novels* (1971). Each story explores the negative repercussions of technological progress—an idea that was in sharp contrast to the technology worship of the space age. One of the novellas had been originally published in 1956; Golding then turned the story into a comedic play titled *The Brass Butterfly,* which was first performed in London in 1958.

Golding's next novel, *Darkness Visible,* appeared in 1979. It addresses the interdependence of good and evil, exemplified in the two main characters: Sophy, who plots to kidnap a child for ransom, and Matty, who gives his life to prevent it.

Golding's 1984 publication, *The Paper Men*, was condemned by reviewers as his worst work, partly because the novel seemed to condemn literary critics. The plot concerns an elderly novelist trying to elude a young scholar who wants to write his biography.

One of Golding's most ambitious works is *The Sea Trilogy,* three full-length novels that follow the emotional education and moral growth of an aristocratic young man named Edmund Talbot during an ocean voyage to Australia in 1812. *Rites of Passage* (1980) shows Talbot's spiritual growth, *Close Quarters* (1987) depicts his emotional and aesthetic development, and *Fire Down Below* (1989) covers his political enlightenment.

Other Work

Golding's work is not limited to fiction: He published three collections of essays which are often comic and expand upon or illuminate his novels. *The Hot Gates and Other Occasional Pieces* was published in 1966; *A Moving Target* appeared in 1982; and *An Egyptian Journal* followed in 1985.

Honors and Awards

Following the publication of his best-known work, *Lord of the Flies*, Golding was granted membership in the Royal Society of Literature in 1955. Ten years later, he received the honorary designation Commander of the British Empire (CBE) and was knighted in 1988. His 1980 novel *Rites of Passage* won the Booker Prize, a prestigious British award. Golding's greatest honor was being awarded the 1983 Nobel Prize for Literature.

INTRODUCTION TO THE NOVEL

The following Introduction section is provided solely as an educational tool and is not meant to replace the experience of your reading the work. Read the Introduction and A Brief Synopsis to enhance your understanding of the work and to prepare yourself for the critical thinking that should take place whenever you read any work of fiction or nonfiction. Keep the List of Characters and Character Map at hand so that as you read the original literary work, if you encounter a character about whom you're uncertain, you can refer to the List of Characters and Character Map to refresh your memory.

Introduction

As all authors use their life and times as reference points in their works, Golding drew heavily on the social-religious-cultural-military ethos of his times. *Lord of the Flies* is an allegorical microcosm of the world Golding knew and participated in. The island and the boys and many other objects and events in the work represent Golding's view of the world and humankind in general and some characteristics or values found in British culture specifically.

Culture and Human Nature

Significant personal life experiences shaped the author and therefore his work. Golding spent two years as a science student at Oxford University before he aborted his pursuit of science for a degree in English literature, his first step toward a rejection of the scientific rationalism espoused by his father. Having joined the British Royal Navy when World War II began, Golding was involved in the invasion of Normandy on D-Day. After his military experience, Golding was a schoolteacher and, for 15 years, immersed himself in reading the Greek classics because, according to him, "this is where the meat is." He felt that Greek drama had a great influence on his work; many scholars agree.

As a synthesis of Golding's life experiences, *Lord of the Flies* investigates three key aspects of the human experience that form the basis of the themes the author wants to convey: (1) The desire for social and political order through parliaments, governments, and legislatures (represented by the platform and the conch). (2) The natural inclination toward evil and violence, manifested in every country's need for a military (represented by the choir-boys-turned-hunters-turned-murderers and in the war going on in the world beyond the island); and (3) The belief in supernatural or divine intervention in human destiny (represented by the ceremonial dances and sacrifices intended to appease the "beast").

By juxtaposing the evil, aggressive nature of the degenerating boys with the proper reserve and civility of the British persona that their cultural background implies, Golding places the boys in a series of life experiences that lead some (like Jack) deeper into their depraved psyche, and some (like Ralph), who recognize the inclination toward evil in themselves, to an epiphany of self-discovery. Such an epiphany is the only hope for humankind to escape from itself.

History

Golding wrote *Lord of the Flies* in 1954, less than a decade after World War II, when the world was in the midst of the Cold War. The atrocities of the Holocaust, the horrific effects of the atomic bomb, and the ominous threat of the Communist demon behind the Iron Curtain were all present in the minds of the western public and the author. This environment of fear combined with technology's rapid advances act as a backdrop to the island experiences: the shot-down plane, for example, and the boys' concern that the "Reds" might find them before the British do.

Historically, in times of widespread socio-economic distress, the general public feels itself vulnerable and turns to the leader who exhibits the most strength or seems to offer the most protection. In *Lord of the Flies*, Jack and the hunters, who offer the luxury of meat and the comforts of a dictatorship, fill that role. In exchange for his protection, the other boys sacrifice any moral reservations they may have about his policies and enthusiastically persecute the boys who resist joining their tribe. These circumstances somewhat mirror Germany's economic suffering, which paved the way for the radical politics of Adolph Hitler's Nazism in the aftermath of World War I and in the worldwide depression of the 1930s.

Based upon his wartime experiences in the British Navy, Golding asserted that the unlimited brutality shown by the Nazis was a capacity not limited to Germans or indeed to any particular group. While the world was horrified by news of the Nazi death camps, Golding felt that none of the nations was too far from committing atrocities of the same magnitude. According to Golding, humankind's propensity toward evil and violence coupled with the "psychology of fear" motivates humanity to act in unconscionable ways. When the United States used the atomic bomb in Japan, more than 100,000 people were killed in three days by dropping two bombs. Overall, a total of 55 million people lost their lives in World War II. Such catastrophic violence and loss of life was clearly not lost on Golding: An atomic war causes the boys' evacuation in *Lord of the Flies*, and the sign from the world of grownups that the boys so wish for turns out to be the body of a dead paratrooper, floating down from an aerial battle.

Sociological/Ideological Concerns

Such a fatalistic view of humanity directly conflicted with the rationalism on which Golding was raised. His father's rationalist optimism held that humankind can be perfected with enough effort, purged of aggressive or anti-social tendencies. Golding's view is much more pessimistic about humankind's true makeup; he perceived human nature as equal parts good and evil, permanently intertwined. Rather than looking to social reform to cure humanity of its cruelty, Golding felt that breakdown in the social order, such as occurs in *Lord of the Flies*, is directly traceable to moral meltdown at the individual's level.

Golding's representation of humanity's inherent evil is a treatment of the Judeo-Christian concept of original sin. When *Lord of the Flies* was published, many critics were not impressed by it because Golding was not part of one of the contemporary literary movements, which concerned themselves not with theology or mysticism but with existential and sociological themes. Instead Golding was a 43-year-old schoolteacher with a wife and children addressing classic themes of good and evil.

As a schoolteacher, however, Golding experienced the reality of schoolboy behavior and tendencies, which provided him with valuable literary material. That reality was quite different from the picture painted in many children's adventure stories, such as R. M. Ballantyne's classic Victorian tale *Coral Island. Coral Island* exemplified certain assumptions about English schoolboys and British culture that Golding knew to be false, such as the idea that British Christian children were naturally virtuous and innocent. Golding wrote *Lord of the Flies* as a solemn parody of *Coral Island,* relocating savagery from the external sources such as heathens and foreigners to residency in each individual's heart.

Another issue Golding addressed was the western world's post-war confidence in technology, another spin on the rationalist idea that human society can be perfected; rationalism's anti-mystical bent is a part of technology worship. Included in the scientific advances of the first half of the twentieth century was the field of psychiatry, which promised to explain emotional disturbances in a logical way—a technology of the mind. Golding wove in references to technology's influence in *Lord of the Flies* through Piggy, who asserts that psychiatry can explain away their fears and that ghosts can't exist because if they did then television and streetlights wouldn't work. While Golding's novel does not prove the existence of ghosts, it does provide a complex commentary on the underlying fears and true demons found in humanity.

A Brief Synopsis

Lord of the Flies explores the dark side of humanity, the savagery that underlies even the most civilized human beings. Golding intended this novel as a tragic parody of children's adventure tales, illustrating humankind's intrinsic evil nature. He presents the reader with a chronology of events leading a group of young boys from hope to disaster as they attempt to survive their uncivilized, unsupervised, isolated environment until rescued.

In the midst of a nuclear war, a group of British boys find themselves stranded without adult supervision on a tropical island. The group is roughly divided into the "littluns," boys around the age of six, and the "biguns," who are between the ages of ten and twelve. Initially, the boys attempt to form a culture similar to the one they left behind. They elect a leader, Ralph, who, with the advice and support of Piggy (the intellectual of the group), strives to establish rules for housing and sanitation. Ralph also makes a signal fire the group's first priority, hoping that a passing ship will see the smoke signal and rescue them. A major challenge to Ralph's leadership is Jack, who also wants to lead. Jack commands a group of choirboys-turned-hunters who sacrifice the duty of tending the fire so that they can participate in the hunts. Jack draws the other boys slowly away from Ralph's influence because of their natural attraction to and inclination toward the adventurous hunting activities symbolizing violence and evil.

The conflict between Jack and Ralph—and the forces of savagery and civilization that they represent—is exacerbated by the boys' literal fear of a mythical beast roaming the island. One night, an aerial battle occurs above the island, and a casualty of the battle floats down with his opened parachute, ultimately coming to rest on the mountaintop. Breezes occasionally inflate the parachute, making the body appear to sit up and then sink forward again. This sight panics the boys as they mistake the dead body for the beast they fear. In a reaction to this panic, Jack forms a splinter group that is eventually joined by all but a few of the boys. The boys who join Jack are enticed by the protection Jack's ferocity seems to provide, as well as by the prospect of playing the role of savages: putting on camouflaging face paint, hunting, and performing ritualistic tribal dances. Eventually, Jack's group actually slaughters a sow and, as an offering to the beast, puts the sow's head on a stick.

Of all the boys, only the mystic Simon has the courage to discover the true identity of the beast sighted on the mountain. After witnessing the death of the sow and the gift made of her head to the beast,

Simon begins to hallucinate, and the staked sow's head becomes the Lord of the Flies, imparting to Simon what he has already suspected: The beast is not an animal on the loose but is hidden in each boy's psyche. Weakened by his horrific vision, Simon loses consciousness. Recovering later that evening, he struggles to the mountaintop and finds that the beast is only a dead pilot/soldier. Attempting to bring the news to the other boys, he stumbles into the tribal frenzy of their dance. Perceiving him as the beast, the boys beat him to death.

Soon only three of the older boys, including Piggy, are still in Ralph's camp. Jack's group steals Piggy's glasses to start its cooking fires, leaving Ralph unable to maintain his signal fire. When Ralph and his small group approach Jack's tribe to request the return of the glasses, one of Jack's hunters releases a huge boulder on Piggy, killing him. The tribe captures the other two biguns prisoners, leaving Ralph on his own.

The tribe undertakes a manhunt to track down and kill Ralph, and they start a fire to smoke him out of one of his hiding places, creating an island-wide forest fire. A passing ship sees the smoke from the fire, and a British naval officer arrives on the beach just in time to save Ralph from certain death at the hands of the schoolboys turned savages.

List of Characters

Ralph The elected leader of the boys and the main protagonist. He is neither the smartest nor the strongest but has a kind of quiet charisma and good looks. He tries to keep the boys focused on domestic order and the rules of civilization but loses his authority and almost his life to Jack's seizure of power.

Piggy Subject of the group's ridicule for his weight, asthma, and general lack of physical prowess or stamina. He provides the brains of the group, as well as the spectacles necessary to start the fire. Loyal to Ralph and all he represents, Piggy's death leaves Ralph alone, pitted in social isolation against Jack's tribe.

Jack Merridew The leader of the choir/hunters. Already militant as a choir leader, Jack leads his group of choirboys-turned-hunters in mutiny against Ralph's leadership by playing on the boys' baser instincts. Jack favors hunting and its savage reward of meat over the civilized domesticity and hope for rescue that Ralph tries to maintain.

Simon The visionary of the group. Given to fainting spells and spending time alone in the jungle, he is considered odd by the other boys. Only Simon understands the true nature of the beast they fear, and only Simon has the courage to investigate the eerie creature sighted on the mountain. Before he can reveal what he has learned, he is killed in a tribal ritual gone too far.

Roger A sly, secretive boy who displays, early on, a cruelty toward the weak and vulnerable. Once joining Jack's tribe, he becomes the hangman, causing Piggy's death, torturing Samneric (Sam and Eric) until they join the tribe, and preparing a stick on which to mount Ralph's head.

Samneric (Sam and Eric) The twin boys who are in charge of keeping the signal fire going. Until they are captured by the tribe, they remain loyal to Ralph. They speak as one, often finishing each other's sentences, so that the other boys pronounce their two names as one word.

Littluns The littlest boys, around ages six and up. They remain with Ralph during the mutiny.

Maurice A bigun who becomes one of Jack's key supporters, accompanying him on the raids on Ralph's camp.

Robert A bigun who plays the role of the pig in one of the tribal dances that reenact a hunt. He is hurt when the dance turns into a fierce beating.

Percival Wemys Madison A littlun who has a nervous breakdown and is often picked on by the other littluns. He introduces the idea that the beast might arrive from the sea.

Johnny One of the smaller littluns who has a mean streak nonetheless.

Henry The biggest of the littluns. He is made the object of a mean-spirited prank by Roger.

Character Map

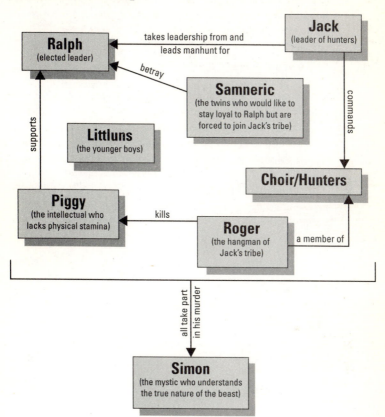

Jack
(leader of hunters)

takes leadership from and
leads manhunt for

Ralph
(elected leader)

betray

Samneric
(the twins who would like to
stay loyal to Ralph but are
forced to join Jack's tribe)

commands

supports

Littluns
(the younger boys)

Choir/Hunters

Piggy
(the intellectual who
lacks physical stamina)

kills

Roger
(the hangman of
Jack's tribe)

a member of

all take part
in his murder

Simon
(the mystic who understands
the true nature of the beast)

CRITICAL COMMENTARIES

The sections that follow provide great tools for supplementing your reading of *Lord of the Flies*. First, in order to enhance your understanding of and enjoyment from reading, we provide quick summaries in case you have difficulty when you read the original literary work. Each summary is followed by commentary: literary devices, character analyses, themes, and so on. Keep in mind that the interpretations here are solely those of the author of this study guide and are used to jumpstart your thinking about the work. No single interpretation of a complex work like *Lord of the Flies* is infallible or exhaustive, and you'll likely find that you interpret portions of the work differently from the author of this study guide. Read the original work and determine your own interpretations, referring to these Notes for supplemental meanings only.

Chapter 1

Summary

Lord of the Flies opens with Ralph meeting Piggy. Their conversation provides the background of their situation: In the midst of a nuclear war, a group of boys was being evacuated to an unnamed destination. Their plane crashed and was dragged out to sea, leaving the boys stranded on an unfamiliar island. Because of the atom bomb's devastation, it's likely that no one knows the boys' whereabouts.

Ralph is delighted to be on a pristine tropical island without adults, but Piggy is less pleased. The two boys make their way out of the jungle and onto the beach. Ralph is not much interested in Piggy and does not request an introduction in turn when Piggy asks Ralph's name. Piggy confides his hope that the boys on this island won't call him Piggy as they did back home.

On the beach, Ralph investigates a large platform of pink granite overlooking a long pool that had formed in the beach. After demonstrating his swimming skills, Ralph spies a conch, which Piggy identifies as a valuable shell that can be blown as a trumpet. Piggy urges Ralph to blow into the shell, using it to summon any other survivors to the beach.

Soon boys between ages 6 and 12 come streaming out of the jungle onto the beach, assembling on the platform near Ralph. Last to arrive are Jack and the choirboys. Despite the tropical heat and their own exertions in following the conch blasts, the boys from the choir still wear their black caps and long black cloaks and are clearly overheated when they reach the platform.

The assembled boys discuss their situation and vote on a chief, choosing Ralph over Jack. Ralph suggests that Jack remain in charge of the choirboys, designating them hunters. Jack is mollified by this seemingly small gift of command. As the assembled boys identify themselves, Ralph reveals Piggy's nickname before Piggy can establish his real name.

Ralph forms a search party to establish that they are, in fact, on an island. In agreeing to go along, Jack reveals with a flourish that he owns a large sheathed knife. Piggy is hurt to be excluded from the search party, and Ralph placates him by giving him the job of taking the names of all the boys who remain behind at the platform.

Ralph, Jack, and Simon confirm that the island is uninhabited. They enjoy their jaunt into the wild, experiencing the thrill of adventure and the new friendship forming between them. On their return, they encounter a piglet trapped in jungle vines, testing Jack's hunting skills and nerve. Jack pulls his knife but falters, and the pig gets away; he vows fiercely that next time he will follow through.

Commentary

Theme

In Chapter 1, Golding introduces the novel's major characters as well as its theme: that evil, as a destructive force in man, society, and civilization, is present in us all. To illustrate this theme, Golding uses several major motifs: civilization versus savagery; humanity versus animality; technology versus nature; hunters versus gatherers; men versus women; adults versus children; and the intellect versus physicality. As the characters interact with each other and with their environment, so do the forces they represent. Using the characters to embody these forces allows Golding the opportunity to compare and contrast with rich shadings of meaning rather than with simplistic oppositions.

The novel opens with a description of the "long scar smashed into the jungle," a reference to the snake-like damage done by the plane as it crashed into the island. Here civilization with its technology has dealt a blow to nature; nature counters by sweeping the wreckage out to sea. Yet the conflict is not so simple. While the jungle may represent nature, the beach provides the conch and the platform, both of which symbolize institutionalized order and politics (civilization).

True to the dynamics of democratic politics, Ralph is elected leader for superficial reasons. He is a personable and handsome boy who appears to be in charge because of his use of the conch, which functions for him at the moment of his election (and throughout the novel) as the symbol of authority. Although it was Piggy's quick thinking to use the conch to summon the others, hampered by asthma, he must allow Ralph to do the summoning. And while Jack clearly has some experience in exerting control over others, making his choirboys march to the assembly through the tropical heat in floor-length black cloaks, the sheer arrogance of his open grab for power probably puts off some of the boys, raised as they have been in a society that values politeness and decorum. Therefore, the boys choose Ralph for his charisma and possession of the compelling conch over Piggy, who lacks the physical stature or char-sima of a leader despite his intelligence, and Jack, who is "ugly without silliness" and possesses a less civil manner.

With his calm, self-assured manner and the poise with which he allows Jack to retain control of the choir and places Piggy in charge of names, Ralph is much more of a diplomat than Jack or Piggy. While allowing Jack control of the hunters turns out to be political (and almost personal) suicide ultimately, Ralph himself is still under the spell of polite society, looking more to make friends than to lead strate-gically. In later chapters, he learns that, as a leader, he must be prepared to take a hard line with his friends if he is to achieve his goals for the group. In Chapter 1, however, Ralph engages in play—standing on his head, blowing jets of water while swimming, rolling a boulder down-hill, gleefully scuffling with Simon—which he has no time for once he is leader of the group.

Note that the talents that set Ralph apart from the others (acrobat-ics and swimming) serve no practical purpose in the jungle, while Jack's recreational activity as choir leader serves him as a leader in training. Jack's warlike nature is evident from the start, as a choirboy who carries a knife and volunteers his choir to be the army, amending its role to hunters at Ralph's direction. While Ralph entertains others with his trick of standing on his head, Jack successfully practices authority: "With dreary obedience" his choir votes for him as chief. He uses to his advantage here his authority, not his ability to sing a C sharp.

From his first appearance as a dark creature, leading his group from the jungle, making them march in columns until Simon faints, Jack is represented as evil. When the creatures turn out to be "a party of boys, marching approximately in step in two parallel lines and dressed in strangely eccentric clothing," Golding is connecting not only the uni-formed military with the frightening dark side of humanity but tac-itly identifying Jack as an outspoken representative of aggression.

Naturally Jack has a strong and vocal aversion to Piggy, who rep-resents thorough domestication in contrast to the savagery lying just beneath Jack's surface. Piggy is no fan of Jack's, being "intimidated by [Jack's] uniformed superiority and the offhand authority in [his] voice." With his poor eyesight, weight problem, and asthma, Piggy is a boy who could survive only in a civilization that offers the dual protection of medical treatment and cultural affluence—a society wealthy enough to provide food, shelter, and purpose for its physically weaker members. In England, Piggy would be valued ultimately for the contribution of his intelligence, despite his lack of physical ability or social skills. On this uninhabited island, however, Piggy is the most vulnerable of all the boys, despite his greater mental capabilities.

Although Ralph treats Piggy badly because Piggy lacks a spirit of adventure, he understands that Piggy has a realistic grasp of their situation. Piggy points out that the atom bomb killed everyone who might know of the boys' whereabouts. While Ralph still speaks of his father in the present tense, telling Piggy that his father will come rescue them soon, Piggy describes his aunt in the past tense, realizing that she is gone. Her voice lives on in his head, however, as the voice that ordered his world and represents the protected domesticity he needs to survive and thrive. His frequent invocations of "my auntie says" provide the only female voice in the book, although he never gets to finish the phrase and reveal what his auntie did say. With only Piggy as her ineffectual mouthpiece, from this first chapter, the auntie's perspective is rendered invalid among the primitive conditions of the environment and the savage demagoguery of Jack.

Character Insight

By quoting his aunt, Piggy also establishes himself as a representative of the adult world. The boys have an ambivalent relationship to adults, viewing them sometimes as providers and protectors and sometimes as punishers and limiters. While Ralph is initially delighted at the lack of grownups on the island, he is at the same time relying on his father's naval expertise to facilitate their rescue. As the adult voice, Piggy tries to communicate the reality that his father is probably dead, a concept that twelve-year-old Ralph has difficulty grasping. Events later in the book reveal Piggy as the voice of reason again—his adult logic contrasting with the other boys' childishly emotional responses, such as in Chapter 2, when he scolds them for starting the fire before building shelters. Yet his logic holds no ground when confronted with the emotions running high in this primitive environment.

Jack and Ralph hold another, more fundamental election between themselves in this chapter. While exploring, they encounter a distinct trail in the jungle. In guessing what made the trail, Ralph offers "'Men?' Jack shakes his head. 'Animals.'" Without realizing it, each boy is casting a vote for who and what they will ultimately represent.

Glossary

>(Here and in the following sections, difficult words and phrases, as well as allusions and historical references, are explained.)

creepers any plants whose stems put out tendrils or rootlets by which the plants can creep along a surface as they grow.

Home Counties the counties nearest London.

stockings closefitting coverings, usually knitted, for the feet and, usually, much of the legs.

half here, considerably; very much.

garter an elastic band, or a fastener suspended from a band, girdle, etc., for holding a stocking or sock in position.

sucks to your auntie a British slang expression of derision or contempt; here, "forget your auntie" or "your auntie be damned."

Gib., Addis abbreviations for Gibraltar and Addis Ababa, respectively; refueling stops the evacuation plane made before crashing on the island.

matins orig., the first of the seven canonical hours, recited between midnight and dawn or, often, at daybreak; here, a morning church service at which the choir sang.

precentor a person who directs a church choir or congregation in singing.

shop here, conversation about one's work or business, esp. after hours.

head boy an honorary title given to a student who has made the best all-around contribution to student life and maintains exemplary conduct.

wacco [Brit. Slang] excellent.

wizard [Brit. Informal] excellent.

smashing [Informal] outstandingly good; extraordinary.

Chapter 2

Summary

Ralph, Jack, and Simon return from their reconnaissance in the late afternoon. Ralph blows the conch to call the other boys back to assembly and describes the results of the exploration. Jack interrupts almost immediately to declare the importance of an army for hunting pigs. So that only one person will speak at a time in the assembly, Ralph makes the conch rule: Only the boy holding the conch can speak, and only Ralph can interrupt the one who holds the conch. Thus, a process for order and civil discourse is established.

Piggy takes the conch so he can make the point that no one knows the boys' location, meaning that they may be on the island a long time. Ralph points out the bright side, the adventure inherent in their situation. At this point the group of littlest boys push a representative forward to describe the "beastie" he saw in the woods the night before; the older boys are quick to assure the littluns that there is no beastie. Ralph offers reassurance that they will definitely be rescued, mentioning that they'll need a signal fire to attract passing ships and planes. At the word fire, Jack immediately takes over the group, leading a charge up the mountain to start a fire. Ralph attempts to maintain order, but everyone rushes after Jack, so he follows, too. Piggy follows last, angry at the impulsive behavior.

On the mountaintop, the boys find a huge patch of dead wood and start a fire, using Piggy's eyeglasses. A massive bonfire that quickly burns itself out results. Jack volunteers his hunters to maintain a signal fire. Suddenly, in the midst of a complaint that no one will let him talk, Piggy sees that they've started a forest fire. He scolds the other boys for their lack of foresight in not first building shelters for the approaching night before racing up the mountain in defiance of Ralph. He further reprimands them for causing not only the waste of so much firewood but also the probable death of some of the littlest boys, since some of them had been playing in the area consumed by the rapidly moving fire. In the face of this news, Ralph attempts to first blame Piggy for not keeping better track of the little boys and then to convince himself and the others that the little ones might have just gone back to the platform. No one is convinced, but all are reluctant to face the reality.

Commentary

Character
Insight

    This chapter continues with and develops the themes established in Chapter 1. Of particular importance to Ralph is his new experience with control over his electorate in the face of political and social dynamics. Initially the boys are quite impressed with him, as he finds he has a natural capacity for public speaking. His promise of rescue seems farfetched given the nuclear war that precipitated the boys' evacuation, but it is a promise he delivers well and believes himself. Even Piggy has faith in Ralph's ability to understand and communicate the issues, although he may be giving him too much credit. When Piggy grabs the conch and says "You're hindering Ralph. You're not letting him get to the most important thing," it's not clear from Ralph's hesitant response that he was in fact going to cover the likelihood that no one knows the boys' location.

    Piggy's loyalty to Ralph stems from Piggy's logical mentality—it's logical to follow the leader's command and assume that he is in control of the situation. The rest of the boys are more emotional. They are quickly swayed from the chief they so respected moments before. Once on the mountain, they are very much impressed by Jack, with his seemingly generous offer to have his hunters take on the fire tending duties, just as they had been enamored of Ralph earlier.

    Such a loyalty shift is part of the dynamics of politics. Golding sums up the status of those who assume a leader's role when he describes the littlest boys' shy representative as "warped out of the perpendicular by the fierce light of publicity." Once an individual such as Jack comes forth and makes himself heard over the rest of the crowd, the crowd views him as larger than life and expects big things—both good and bad. Leaders often attain a level of celebrity, at which point both their faults and their virtues are magnified by publicity's distorting lens so that their smallest mistakes may be viewed by the public with the same importance granted their greatest achievements. This syndrome springs from the emotional reaction that leaders invoke.

Character
Insight

    Piggy is missing this emotional connection. He may be attempting to present the most beneficial plan of action for the group, but, because he lacks rapport with the other boys, he cannot make himself heard. Seeing that the boys pay attention to Ralph when he repeats what Piggy has already tried to communicate, he protests "'That's what I said! I said about the meetings and things and then you said shut up—.' His voice lifted into the whine of virtuous recrimination. They stirred and began to shout him down." Piggy realizes the effect he has on the boys but not the cause of it, placing too much faith in the logical approach. Truth is not always obvious, and logic is seldom universal. Not until Piggy loses his temper can he get the boys' attention and reveal the priorities he had in mind before they raced up the mountain. He points out that the island gets cold at night and that they should have built shelters before nightfall, his reason expressed too late for their emotional deeds.

Theme

Piggy also relies too heavily on the power of the conch, on the social convention that holding the conch invests him with the right to be heard. He believes that upholding social conventions gets results. "How can you expect to be rescued if you don't . . . act proper?" Piggy asks. He is partially right but is overlooking the dynamic of the crowd, the emotionality of mob rule. When Piggy screams, "You'll break the conch!" he is in essence protesting "you'll break the covenant," the agreement that everyone will behave in a certain way and follow established rules. The rules are more immediately necessary for him than for the other boys who can rely on their physical skills to survive.

Literary Device

Jack's rush up the mountain shatters the power of the conch rule, which is meant to ensure civil, rational conversation. Jack asserts that the conch has no power once they are on the mountain, but clearly it didn't have that much power on the platform either: Ralph shouted for order while holding the conch but lost the crowd in the excitement, foreshadowing how later he loses his authority completely. The impulsive dash with which Jack leads the boys away from the platform symbolizes the ease with which humanity's emotional, savage nature overwhelms its rational and civilized tendencies.

Literary Device

To represent the evil that is part of human nature, Golding uses the beastie described by the littlest boys. At night, they report, the beast lurks in the jungle hunting and looking to devour them; by day it disguises itself as the creeper vines that hang innocently in the trees. Here the vines are like human nature in the daylight of civilization; in the darkness of a primeval environment their true predatory nature emerges. During the forest fire, the little boys shriek at the burning creeper vines "Snakes! Snakes! Look at the snakes!" This allusion is to the serpent in the Garden of Eden who stole innocence and introduced humanity to its own physicality.

Theme

Obviously on a conscious level, the boys perceive this beast as an actual animal rather than as the conceptualization of the evil inherent in humanity. Yet these littlest boys have an immediate and instinctive recognition of the island as a threat to them: They realize that they lack the domesticity that protected them back home. The older boys ostensibly reject the little boys' fear, presenting the logical explanation that the island is too small for large predators. Ralph is vehement on this point: "Something he had not known was there rose in him and compelled him to make the point, loudly and again. 'But I tell you there isn't a beast!'" He is denying that there exists a dark side to humanity.

Literary Device

The fire on the mountain has tremendous symbolic meaning. First, it represents hope and aspirations for the future, a gift from the gods, a tool that separates humankind from the animals. Just as the beach platform and the untamed jungle represent the duality in humanity's behavior, the fire, also, represents both savagery (evil) and hope: "On one side the air was cool, but on the other the fire thrust out a savage arm of heat." Golding could be describing here how societies and individuals contain these conflicting yet complementary forces. In some individuals, the savage side runs closer to the surface, as with Jack, but it exists in everyone. The boys' fire shows that one entity can contain hot and cold, good and evil, civility and savagery.

The fire expresses another duality as well, a before and after for Ralph's perception of their situation and his role. This first bonfire is an act of communal play for all the boys, topped off with Ralph standing on his head to mark their triumph. The fire becomes more like serious work when they make plans for specific teams to tend it. Later, with the probable deaths of some of the little boys, Ralph begins to realize that the group's disregard for his authority can and will have grim consequences. Before the fire, the boys take time for play, a luxury available only to those protected by a civilization, not for those engaged in a fight for survival.

Literary Device

Ultimately, the fire is about savagery: For the boys rushing around for firewood, "Life became a race with the fire," a phrase that quietly foreshadows Ralph's flight for his life at the end. And while fire starting was one of the first technologies to separate humanity from the animals, to start this fire, the boys adopt a primitive use of force in taking Piggy's glasses from him, making him an unwilling Prometheus.

Note that on this first day together, the group has already banded together to physically overwhelm Piggy—a show of physicality over intellect. It is also an uprising of children against an adult figure. Although Piggy is in the same age group as the other boys, he nonetheless holds the role of "martyred . . . parent who has to keep up with the senseless ebullience of the children." On this island, for the first time in their lives, the boys experience sheer autonomy. "This is our island . . . . Until the grownups come and fetch us, we'll have fun," Ralph says, in an utterly failed and foolish prophecy.

By now the reader is aware of many of the developing symbols in the story:

■   Ralph, the responsible leader who attempts to organize the boys for their survival and rescue. He appears practical, capable of using Piggy's advice, able to avoid superstition and fear, and capable of developing processes for advancing their limited society.

■   Jack, the evil that lurks within humankind, the one most in tune with his primitive urges and instincts.

■   Piggy, the intellectual who is physically inept, the least capable of surviving on this island under these circumstances.

■   Simon, the artistic, sensitive mystic.

■   The conch, representing authority and civil debate.

■   The snake-like images (the scar left by the passenger tube, the "creepers" [vines] that are encountered throughout), representing aggression, fear, and evil.

Glossary

Treasure Island   Robert Louis Stevenson's 1883 novel about a heroic boy's search for buried gold and his encounter with pirates.

Swallows and Amazons   the first (1930) of a series of adventure books by Arthur Ransome, about a group of children on vacation.

Coral Island Robert Ballantyne's 1857 adventure tale about three boys shipwrecked on a Pacific island and their triumph over their circumstances.

caps of maintenance caps bearing a school insignia.

altos the boys who sing in the vocal range between tenor and soprano.

trebles the boys who sing the highest part in musical harmony.

Chapter 3

Summary

Jack, alone on a pig hunt, has clearly learned some tracking techniques. Frustrated that his day's hunt has ended yet again without a kill, he returns from the jungle to the area where Ralph and Simon work on building shelters.

Ralph expresses his frustration: Although all the boys have agreed to help build shelters, only Simon actually puts in the time and effort alongside Ralph. All the other boys are off playing, bathing, or hunting with Jack, even though Jack and his hunters have failed so far to produce meat. Ralph emphasizes the need for sturdy shelters, while Jack insists that he and the other boys need meat and tries to explain his compulsion to hunt. This difference—and the undercurrent of rancor—makes both boys uncomfortable given the relationship that had sprung up between them on the first day's exploring adventure.

Also in this chapter, a new side of Simon is revealed. He has a secret place in the jungle, a sort of hut formed by vines, boulders, and trees. After helping Ralph with the shelters all day, he sneaks off to this shelter, pausing first to help the littluns gather some choice fruit and making sure that he hasn't been followed.

Commentary

Theme

In the first two chapters, Golding established regulated speech as a hallmark of civilization, as the boys set up the platform as a site for assemblies ordered by the conch. Ralph uses the conch to mimic the practice of "hands up," which all the boys know from school, the very place where literacy and verbal communication is systematically developed. In this chapter, Golding further develops this theme: Whereas verbal language is the sole property of civilization, silence is a property of nature. As Jack hunts in the "uncommunicative forest," he finds the "silence of the forest was more oppressive than the heat."

Ironically, when, in this chapter, Jack encounters Ralph at the shelters, Ralph comments on the uselessness of talk, railing about the abandoned resolutions to work everyone voices at the assemblies. "Meetings. Don't we love meetings?" Ralph says bitterly, confused by the assemblies' lack of efficacy. He had been counting on the meetings to provide both framework and impetus for focused action but has found that, of a crowd, only a few actually follow through. Ralph's vision of order is one most of the other boys share but lack the self-discipline to carry out. With language as his only tool, Ralph's authority lacks the threat possessed by parents and schoolmasters to enforce the rules and resolutions. Although he doesn't like building huts any better than any of the others, he is able to control his impulses and do what is necessary.

Character Insight

Jack could serve as an enforcer of rightful authority and necessary discipline, but he does not share Ralph's civilized vision. He is fast losing the traces of civilization and tuning into his animal self: crouched "dog-like" and reacting to a sudden bird cry with "a hiss of indrawn breath . . . ape-like among the tangle of trees." Jack seems to be losing his powers of rational thought, as well: Not only does he not share Ralph's priority on rescue, he "had to think for a moment before he could remember what rescue was." In trying to explain his feeling of being hunted while on the hunt, he finds verbalizing his experiences a great effort. The ability to express himself verbally is a skill necessary to civilization, not to hunting. His efforts go now to communicating with the nonverbal jungle, reading the signs left by the pigs. Where as Ralph can control his impulses for the good of the community, Jack puts all his focus on developing his impulses—in this case, his need to hunt.

Furthermore, neither boy can communicate his perspective to the other, and neither considers the other's viewpoint. This lack of communication underlies innumerable conflicts, and the lack of understanding frequently has more to do with unwillingness on the listener's part than on the speaker's. Ralph and Simon's reactions to Jack's revelation about feeling hunted while hunting are true to form for both of them.

When Jack tries to convey his experience of the beast, he meets with resistance from Ralph. As the representative of reasonable society, Ralph is "incredulous and faintly indignant" that Jack could be granting any credit to the idea of a beast. Ralph is either unable or unwilling to acknowledge the existence of a beast. In contrast, the mystic visionary

Simon is "intent" on understanding how Jack's feeling corresponds with the intuitive knowledge Simon has of human nature. Like the littluns, Jack's sense of the beast is formless and inarticulate; his domain is the emotions, which rule and fuel his animal nature. In truth, Jack *is* being hunted, in a sense, and both he and Simon, to varying degrees, recognize this. Ralph can't acknowledge this and continue to believe in what he believes in and relies on: the basic civility of man.

Character Insight

This chapter reveals Simon as the mystic. While Golding doesn't specify why Simon has a secret place or what he does there, clearly Simon feels the need to be sheltered from the other boys. "He's queer. He's funny," says Ralph of his only work partner, which is the reaction mystics typically provoke from mainstream society. Simon is different from the other boys not only due the physical frailty of fainting spells but also in his consistently expressed concern for the other more vulnerable boys. In the previous chapter, he sticks up for Piggy when Jack verbally attacks him for not gathering firewood, pointing out that the fire was started with Piggy's glasses. In this chapter, Simon takes the time to pluck from the trees the choice fruits that the littluns can't reach and passing them down "to the endless, outstretched hands," an almost saintly image.

Style & Language

Simon's role as a visionary is alluded to in this chapter not only by his hidden place of meditation but also by Golding's description of his eyes: "so bright they had deceived Ralph into thinking him delightfully gay and wicked." While Piggy has the glasses, another symbol of vision, Simon has the bright eyes that later in the novel see the truth about the beast.

To highlight Ralph's growing disenchantment with Jack and disillusionment with being a leader, Golding brings back together, in this chapter, the three boys who went exploring that first day. Caught up in the glamour of newness and adventure, the three seemed to become instant friends. By now, however, Ralph cannot overlook that Jack's priority on hunting is undermining his own efforts to create a home for the boys, that Simon is not the mischievous prankster Ralph perceived him to be, and that the boys in general quickly forget their promises to work toward a common goal when faced with the more immediate gratification of eating and playing. Ralph has come to the realization that "people were never quite what you thought they were."

Glossary

batty [Slang] crazy or eccentric.

crackers [Slang, Chiefly Brit.] crazy; insane.

queer differing from what is usual or ordinary; odd; singular; strange.

Chapter 4

Summary

The chapter opens with a general description of the island's changes throughout the day and the boys' responses to each day's cyclical progression. The focus narrows to the littluns' subculture and three of the littluns interacting as they play with one of their sandcastles. Then Roger and Maurice emerge from the jungle and deliberately destroy some of the sandcastles on their way to the beach.

Jack gathers the hunters to reveal his new hunting strategy: using colored clay and charcoal to camouflage their faces. Jack commands all his hunters, including Samneric who are on fire-maintenance duty at the time, to join in a hunt.

Ralph spots a ship in the distance and is confident that the ship's crew will spot the boys' smoke signal. But, unknown to Ralph, the fire has gone out, being left unattended. When Simon points out that there is no smoke, he and Ralph and Piggy hurry up the mountainside. By the time all three have reached the dormant fire site, the ship is gone.

Meanwhile, Jack and his hunters are triumphant, marching up to the fire site with the carcass of a pig. Jack and Ralph face off about the desertion of the fire for the sake of the hunt. Jack apologizes but Ralph remains angry. Tensions ease somewhat as the boys eat roast pig. The hunters reenact the kill as a sort of celebratory dance. In response, Ralph announces an assembly on the platform immediately.

Commentary

Style & Language

As the most fundamental of all cycles, the daily experience of morning's promise followed inevitably by night's menace is a microcosm of larger cycles. Golding's opening description of the island's daily rhythm is evocative of the many cycles that govern humanity: the life of an individual from birth to death, the development and disintegration of cultures, the rise and fall of great civilizations.

Even among this small group of boys, subcultures have sprung up. The littluns spend their days among themselves, following their own priorities and interests; "their passionately emotional and corporate life was their own." Within the littluns are further distinctions based on size and temperament, either of which can provide an immediate advantage to one littlun over another: "Henry was a bit of a leader this afternoon, because the other two were Percival and Johnny, the smallest boys on the island." Yet Johnny has the upper hand over the sensitive Percival due to his inclination to bully. In addition, while Johnny may be one of the smallest, he is also "well built." With no adults to control their activities, Henry and Johnny join in picking on Percival because they enjoy the thrill of mastery over another creature and because it keeps boredom at bay.

Literary Device

The boys focus on the most entertaining possibilities of the island, such as hunting, playing, and eating, to the detriment of such mundane but necessary tasks as building shelters. They are free to set their own priorities and agenda on an individual basis, allowing some of the boys the chance to develop the application of their own worst impulses. Henry, for example, assumes a dictatorial manner, experimenting further with mastery over other creatures as he traps tiny transparent beach scavengers in his footprints. His experience is a microcosm of another kind: Describing how Henry "became absorbed beyond happiness as he felt himself exercising control over living things," Golding alludes not only to Henry and Johnny's persecution of Percival but also to Jack's compulsion to hunt and to the probable cause of the nuclear war that landed the boys on this island.

The link between Henry's activities and Jack's is further strengthened by the image of Henry's attempt to verbally control the transparent creatures—"He talked to them, urging them, ordering them"—which evokes the image of Jack in the previous chapter staring at the traces of the pig trail "as though he would force them to speak to him." Both boys try to force their verbal communication on nonverbal entities, an effort doomed to failure. Henry cherishes what little control he feels he has and does not mind that his orders go unheeded. His efforts at mastery over another are still in the play stage, although cruel nonetheless to the vulnerable Percival. Jack, on the other hand, has a much more difficult time tolerating resistance. When the boys are forced to rebuild the fire in a different spot because Ralph silently refuses to move from the site of the original fire, Jack is furious. Ralph uses a means of control over the group that is nonverbal and nonviolent, ensuring that neither the rhetorical skills nor the physical superiority of the hunters can be used against him. In the face of passive resistance, Jack is powerless to stop Ralph from imposing his will on the group and asserting his authority.

As the biguns Roger and Maurice torment the littluns by destroying their sandcastles, they still hear in their heads the reprimanding adult voices of the civilization they left behind. Roger throws rocks at Henry, but he throws them so that they'll miss, surrounded as Henry is by "the protection of parents and school and policeman and the law. Roger's arm was conditioned by a civilization that knew nothing of him and was in ruins."

Character Insight

Even Jack still feels the influence of his former life, laughing while he describes the great amounts of blood spilled in the hunt but shuddering at the same time. His distaste is followed quickly by acceptance, however, as he wipes his bloody hands on his shorts. Golding implies a certain relief for Jack in the phrase "able at last to hit someone, [Jack] stuck his fist into Piggy's stomach." His entire life had been moderated by rules set by adults against hitting other children or physically acting out his aggression; now on the island, only the conditioning he received while still in civilization holds him back, and the imprint of that conditioning is fading fast from his character.

Most societies judge character to a great extent by how an individual behaves, how thoroughly a person has internalized the mores and ethos of civilized society. British culture, in particular, places a high value on maintaining civility even under adverse circumstances, the mask of good manners concealing strong emotions and impulses. Jack discovers the other side of a mask's power—the power to liberate—when he applies the clay and charcoal camouflage: "the mask was a thing on its own, behind which Jack hid, liberated from shame and self-consciousness."

While the masks of polite society leash our evil nature, Jack's mask of colored clay unleashes it. The mask—or the transformation it invokes—frightens the hunter Bill, who initially laughs but then backs off into the jungle, and it compels the twins to abandon their fire tending duties, a symbol of how they are being drawn away from all of the civilized domesticity and communal hope for rescue represented by the fire. Jack refers to the mask as "dazzle paint," the camouflage used in warfare, clearly linking his new identity as a shameless killer with those adults fighting the war.

Character Insight

When the ship is sighted, Ralph remains calmly in place while the other boys present blunder around in excitement. Yet, when he realizes that there is no smoke signal for the ship to sight, he loses the calm that has so far characterized his behavior—the mask over his emotions. Now he rushes heedlessly up to mountain to the fire site, "savaging himself" on the bushes, reaching the top only to see that the fire is out and the ship is leaving. He loses control at this point: "his voice rose insanely. 'Come back! Come back!' . . . Ralph reached inside himself for the worst word he knew. 'They let the bloody fire go out.'" His use of a profanity indicates strong emotion not yet displayed; his anger compels him to break with the decorum so important to his culture. In the midst of this crisis, even Piggy, who is most closely linked with adult perspectives, "whimper[s] like a littlun" when he reaches the mountain top and, in the next chapter, also uses a vulgarity when Simon suggests that there may be a beast.

Style & Language

Under duress, some of the boys break with the social decorum expected of the offspring of proper civility, letting their baser emotions rule. Others of the boys go further, abandoning rational thought or civil communication. Jack has begun to think like an animal, as when he explains his rationale for the dazzle paint. His speech pattern becomes simplistic, mimicking the impressionistic understanding of animals: "They see me, I think. Something pink, under the trees." His group of hunters doesn't have the mechanism of the conch to regulate their discourse; they talk over each other when describing their successful hunt. When Jack as leader wants to make himself heard, he interrupts and takes the floor by force of personality rather than by an established, polite precedent.

Jack's shortsightedness has cost the boys a rescue while at the same time bringing them the immediate victory of a kill. Firmly rooted in their respective worlds, neither Ralph nor Jack can understand the other's position. "There was the brilliant world of hunting, tactics, fierce exhilaration, skill; and there was the world of longing and baffled common-sense." When Ralph denounces Jack for not keeping his agreement to maintain the fire, he is mourning not merely the lost opportunity for rescue but the loss of the world they've left behind in England. Because Jack has already lost interest in that world of politeness and boundaries, he feels no compunction to keep the fire going or to attend to any of the other responsibilities of a domestic life. He uses the device of an apology as a tool to end the conflict with Ralph, more of an instinctive political maneuver than an expression of regret. This apology pleases the crowd but infuriates Ralph, who perceives the apology as a "verbal trick" distracting everyone from the tragedy that had just occurred. Rhetoric triumphs for Jack despite the harm he has caused with his negligence and misplaced priorities.

Later, after Simon rebukes Jack for refusing Piggy a share of the meat, Jack lists all he has done to bring the boys meat in an effort to gain their full appreciation for his accomplishment and for what he's going through in his metamorphosis from choirboy to killer. The others do not fully comprehend Jack's message. He "looked round for understanding but found only respect." Although he does not get understanding, he does get respect, which is all that is required for a demagogue. Jack also discovers that the ritualistic face-painting and dancing further separates him from the constraints of his civil training and that involving his hunters in the dancing and chanting of the mock hunt after the meal has a powerful bonding effect, bringing the hunters more strongly under his influence.

Ralph is envious of this influence and of the victory Jack has brought to the group. He has not been able to provide such a decisive triumph for the boys, dependent as his agenda is on the external event of rescue and on the maintenance of cultural norms alien to their current environment. When he announces an immediate assembly, he is calling the boys not only to the platform but back to all that it symbolizes.

Glossary

dazzle paint British term for camouflage; the disguising of troops, ships, guns, etc. to conceal them from the enemy, as by the use of paint, nets, or leaves in patterns merging with the background.

accent a distinguishing regional or national manner of pronunciation; here, Piggy's manner of speech, characterized by his use of double negatives and informal contractions.

bloody [Vulgar Brit. Slang] cursed; damned.

Ha'porth contraction of "a halfpenny's worth," meaning a very small amount.

One for his nob a hit on his head.

Give him a fourpenny one hit him on the jaw.

Chapter 5

Summary

Ralph calls the assembly and reminds everyone of their agreement to maintain fresh water supplies, observe sanitation measures, build shelters, and keep the signal fire going. He then addresses the growing fear that he knows is beginning to overwhelm many of the boys by opening up the floor for discussion. Meanwhile, darkness is falling.

Jack takes the conch to point out that if a beast were on the island, he would have seen it during his hunting trips. Piggy adds that the field of psychology can be used as a tool to explain logically the experience of fear, thereby invalidating it. When a littlun comes forward to describe a large creature he saw in the jungle the night before, Simon reveals that it was only he, going to his special place. Percival suggests that a beast could arise from the sea, then falls asleep on the platform from the effort of his revelation.

Simon attempts to explain that the boys themselves, or something inherent in human nature, could be the beast they fear. His unsuccessful explanation leads to talk of ghosts, so Ralph holds a vote to see who fears ghosts. This vote sparks an outburst from the rational Piggy with a corresponding reaction from Jack. Now in open mutiny, Jack aggressively disputes Ralph's authority and leads the boys onto the beach in a sort of tribal dance. Remaining on the platform, Piggy and Simon urge Ralph to summon everyone back to the platform but he resists, his confidence shaken. Suddenly, the three boys are startled by an unearthly wail as Percival wakes up to find himself alone in the dark.

Commentary

Chapter 3 addresses the issue of verbal communication and its place within a civilized society; this chapter implies that the primitive life leaves little mental energy for conceptual thought. Making his way to the platform, Ralph realizes "the wearisomeness of this life, where . . . a considerable part of one's waking life was spent watching one's feet." With so much energy devoted to survival, little time is left to devote to the kind of conceptual thought or abstract reasoning available to those sheltered by the institutions found in civilizations.

Theme

The two boys who retain the most capacity for conceptual thought are Piggy and Simon. Note that Piggy does not participate in the physical endeavors of the other boys; his physical activities are limited by his poor physical condition. Simon makes the effort to be alone in his hidden spot, giving himself time to meditate in a place where he doesn't have to concern himself with hunting, building, or the needs of others. In the hidden spot, Simon develops his understanding of human nature as the true beast to be feared.

The silence of Simon's hideaway allows him to reflect on what he sees and feels. In contrast, silence is a threat to the other boys. Consider Jack's feeling oppressed by the jungle's silence while hunting in Chapter 3. During the assembly in this chapter, the boys respond almost aggressively to Percival's silence when asked his name: "Tormented by the silence and the refusal the assembly broke into a chant. 'What's your name? What's your name?'" Chanting is associated with primitive societies, not part of the order or domesticity from whence the boys came or that Ralph is trying to establish.

Character Insight

Ralph expends much energy on the needs of others as well as on the physical rigors of building huts, and he begins to feel the effects: He is gradually losing both confidence that they will be rescued and his feeling that they are involved in an exciting experiment without adults. As a boy who represents the civilized, English society, he is neither as savage as Jack nor as cerebral as Piggy. He provides an example of how the leader in a community must strive to utilize the intellectual resources available in solving communal problems. This chapter shows Ralph's skills of organization and governance starting to wane. He is struggling to implement his agenda for the meeting and finds he is unable to control the assembly, which degenerates into a mob of "noise and excitement, scramblings, screams and laughter." He finds himself lost "in a maze of thoughts that were rendered vague by his lack of words to express them." This lack of mental clarity recalls Jack's difficulty in expressing himself described in Chapter 3. Such a loss of verbal command bodes ill for Ralph and the community because his seat of authority is the platform, a symbol of the verbal communication and thoughtful debate. Ralph's mental acumen is subject to the same decay as his clothing, frayed as both are by the rigors of the primitive life.

Yet the crisis of the lost rescue opportunity spurs Ralph to grasp some new concepts, revelations following each other thick and fast as he makes his way to the platform and sits on the chief's log. His growth is evident in his musings as he ponders matters more conceptual than he ever has before. Realizing the difficulty of this lifestyle in contrast to its initial glamour, he "smiled jeeringly," as an adult might look back with cynicism on the ideals held as a youth. Ralph is losing his innocence quickly, but gaining an understanding of natural processes not available to him in the sheltered society he came from. "With a convulsion of the mind, Ralph discovered dirt and decay . . . At that he began to trot" toward the platform and the civilization it represents, in a physical reaction to the abstract truth newly present within him.

Once on the platform, more revelations engulf Ralph. He considers the springy log that shifts during assemblies and throws off the boys sitting on it, and ponders how maintenance of the status quo has taken precedence over the simple solution of securing the log with a stone wedge. He notes that the light of late sunset makes the entire place look different, calling into question the reality of its usual appearance. Suddenly Ralph recognizes the value and talents of the intellectually gifted Piggy, a conscious appreciation foreshadowed by the allegiance formed in Chapter 4 when "Not even Ralph knew how a link between him and Jack had been snapped and fastened elsewhere." At the same time, Ralph realizes that "Piggy was no chief," understanding intuitively that a leader needs the popular support Piggy can't garner, hindered by his lack of charisma or popular appeal.

Up to this point, Ralph himself has been leading by instinct and charisma. Now he realizes that "if you were a chief, you had to think, you had to be wise . . . thought was a valuable thing, that got results." Simultaneously, he realizes "I can't think. Not like Piggy." This sentiment echoes Piggy's question to the boys in Chapter 2, after they've accidentally caused the forest fire: "How can you expect to be rescued if you don't . . . act proper?" In that scenario, Piggy links social conventions with results, in a logical relationship of cause and effect lost on the emotional crowd. Social conventions are not necessarily based in rational thought, but they do provide a framework for rational discussion and thought.

Ralph has clearly learned something about establishing a forum for discussion: "One had to sit, attracting all eyes to the conch, and drop words like heavy round stones among the little groups that crouched or squatted." Golding's word choices here evoke a distinct sense of primitivism, a savage lifestyle where words are stones and the chief presides over an electorate that crouches and squats to hear him speak. Just as Chapter 4 lays out a series of microcosms with the littluns' interactions, the diction here links the platform assemblies to both ends of the social or civil spectrum, from pre-verbal tribe gatherings to modern governmental institutions.

With hunting, Jack has a skill that is becoming increasingly more persuasive to the group in their present environment than does Ralph. Jack's appeal to the primitive, baser, instinctive nature of the community, coupled with his aggressive, self-assured combative personality, is now appealing more and more to the group. At the same time, Ralph's political and natural leadership abilities coupled with his visceral optimism and common sense are having diminishing impact on the affairs of the boys as their baser natures become increasingly prevalent.

In this chapter's assembly, Ralph's new appreciation for thought leads him to rely too heavily on logic. While he presents his agenda point by point, attempting a rational approach to the fear he knows they feel, night is falling and the boys are growing restless. "We've got to talk about this fear and decide there's nothing in it," he says, as if a phobia can be defused through discussion. As the brainy representative of civilization, Piggy continues along these utterly rational lines. "'Life,' said Piggy expansively, 'is scientific'" in his explanation that such an emotional concern can be addressed as a pathology with the twentieth-century invention of psychology. His assertion that soon humankind would by flying to Mars indicates his confidence in technology, which he holds out as a source of comfort.

Yet Jack provides the most comfort to the boys in this assembly because he portrays the object of their fear as an actual animal, one that can be tracked, and "[t]he whole assembly applauded him with relief" when he points out that he has never seen a frightening beast of any kind in the forest; his skills as a tracker are undeniable. Jack orders everyone to be frightened if they must—he acknowledges that even he feels that same fear at times—but not to fear an animal-beast. Jack pleases the crowd with his practical take on the beast and his definitive pronouncement that "you'll have to put up with [the fear] just like the rest of us."

Given the day's lost rescue opportunity, Ralph implements the additional precaution of using only the signal fire to cook rather than starting small wasteful fires on the beach—an idea that is solidly grounded in reality. Still counting on logic to carry his agenda, Ralph points out

"You voted me for chief. Now you do what I say." Ralph thus raises the issue of the electorate's obligation to the rule. Winning of public opinion is both a reasoned and an emotionally based process. Every politician knows that popular opinion is easily swayed from one leader to another; the general public's perception of who is the best leader is frequently based not on which leader has benefited the group the most, but who has gained favor most recently. Already, Ralph's authority has lost ground, due to the concrete victory of a kill offered by Jack, the adventure and drama of the hunts, and the overall emotional nature of a crowd.

Ralph, Piggy, and Simon assume that adults could solve the problems they face on the island. After the assembly, the three boys detail the advantages adults bring, crediting adults with the greatest efficacy and civility: "Grownups know things . . . They ain't afraid of the dark. They'd meet and have tea and discuss. Then things @'ud be all right." Ralph has been trying to uphold that model, using discussion as a means to set things right, but this chapter sees him lose faith in it. When the other boys have been once again led off by Jack, Ralph cannot bring himself to summon them back.

Although Piggy is an undoubted representative of logic and science, he is the first to address the idea that the fear could be based on a fear of self and each other, of something inherent in humanity. Piggy developed his shrewd understanding of human nature during the time spent bedridden by asthma—the equivalent for him of Simon's secret place in the jungle. For Piggy, the fear is less a concept rooted in knowledge of humanity's dark side than the practical fear of an outsider, a vulnerable boy disliked by the stronger, more aggressive boys.

Character Insight

Like Piggy, Simon is different from the others: He has fainting spells, sticks up for Piggy even if unobtrusively, and has the special hidden place in the forest; later chapters reveal him as a visionary. Because the other boys don't understand Simon, they fear him. When he reveals that it was he who inadvertently frightened one of the littluns by venturing into the jungle at night, he gives them a concrete reason to chastise him. Jack holds him up for ridicule; the "derisive laughter that rose had fear in it and condemnation"—two emotions that go hand in hand as the condemnation makes the group feel protected from the fear they've experienced.

Literary Device

Simon's death is foreshadowed in this chapter, as he is made scapegoat for the boys' unshakeable fear. His question to them, "What's the dirtiest thing there is?" demands an answer far too abstract for this crowd. Once again, Jack provides a concrete and non-threatening answer, an answer far simpler than the answer Simon seeks, which is evil. Simon can't express precisely what he understands because he lacks a sophisticated education or training in dealing with abstract concepts; he is, after all, a ten-year-old boy. Simon's inability to articulate what he sees as "mankind's essential illness" mirrors Jack's inability to effectively express "the compulsion to track down and kill that was swallowing him up." Both boys want to describe the same thing, but Simon has reached an abstract understanding of the animality that can produce evil effects while Jack is living it. Of course, Jack later stirs up the group into such a frenzy of animality that Simon is murdered.

Theme

This chapter expands upon the theme of humankind's latent depravity, resorting to the savagery of self-indulgence in the absence of social rules, mores, and control to the contrary. Such control is the basis of most social conventions and institutions, which are designed to promote self-control and civilized discourse. The symbol of such conventions and institutions is the platform. In this chapter the platform's protective powers break down when the assembly dissolves into "arguing, gesticulating shadows. To Ralph, seated, this seemed the breaking up of sanity." When Ralph sees the disorderly arguing breaking out and taking over the assembly, he perceives not only that he has lost control of the group but that the group is losing control of itself.

Glossary

lavatory [Chiefly Brit.] a flush toilet.

taken short informal phrase for having diarrhea.

jolly [Brit. Informal] very; altogether.

bogie an imaginary evil being or spirit; goblin.

mucking about [Slang, Chiefly Brit.] wasting time; puttering around.

sod you a vulgar British slang phrase showing extreme contempt.

nuts a slang exclamation of disgust, scorn, disappointment, refusal, etc.

bollocks a vulgar slang exclamation expressing anger, disbelief, etc.

Chapter 6

Summary

After the assembly, all the boys go to sleep. Above them an aerial battle is taking place. A casualty of the battle floats down to the island on his opened parachute. The wind drags the body to rest at the top of the mountain. The breeze inflates the parachute occasionally, making the body appear to sit up and then sink forward again. Samneric, tending the fire on the mountain, catch a glimpse of the body's movement and hear the parachute inflating. They flee to Ralph in a panic with a story exaggerated by their fear.

At dawn, Ralph calls an assembly, where they decide to investigate the only spot on the island left unexplored: the castle-like rock formation at one end. With Piggy and the littluns remaining behind on the beach, Ralph and the others go to the castle. Ralph goes first by himself, followed a few minutes later by Jack. After they establish that the beast is not there, the other boys join them in the castle and want to play there a while. They resist when Ralph announces that they need to all go check on the fire, but he forces the issue and Jack leads the way back up to the fire site.

Commentary

This chapter begins and ends ominously. The aerial battle that opens the chapter establishes that war continues to rage in the world where most of the boys long to return. Ralph, Piggy, and Simon finished the previous chapter detailing the merits of adults and adult behavior, how adults would remedy their unpleasant situation with ease and dignity. Yet that night, "a sign came down from the world of grownups" that is frightening and mysterious and changes the entire complexion of the group for the worse. When Samneric establish to everyone's satisfaction that an actual beast does exist, the boys shift automatically and instinctively into an aggressive mode based on fear: "the circle began to change. It faced out, rather than in, and the spears of sharpened wood were like a fence."

The main theme of this chapter is the effect of fear. For Samneric, their initial fright magnifies their involvement with the creature from merely seeing movement and hearing the parachute to being actively chased down the mountain as they flee. They report eyes, teeth, and claws that they couldn't possibly have seen. The other boys are so eager for a remedy to this fear that they feel the first unified urge for mutiny when Ralph forces them to leave the perceived safety of the fort-like castle rock to check on the fire.

Fear acts as a sort of litmus test for leadership. While Piggy and Jack both put forth unworkable plans of action—Piggy wanting to restrict their living area to the platform, Jack wanting to rush out and hunt the beast down—Ralph is able to proceed with sense and caution. Harkening back to his new appreciation for the power of thought, Ralph lays out his concerns about both plans and asserts, "So we've got to think." He points out that the beast obviously can't be hunted like the pigs because it leaves no tracks; otherwise, Jack would have already seen the tracks. Remaining all the time on the platform will not work due to lack of fire, food, and space. Ralph is able to keep the group's focus on the hope for rescue, despite Jack's attack on his authority.

Fear brings out the dictator in Jack. He attempts to take control of the group, claiming this situation is "a hunter's job" in which Ralph is not qualified to command. Showing yet again no mercy for the help-less or vulnerable, he advocates abandoning the littluns without a guardian while everyone else goes on the hunt. Like a dictator, he assigns a high value only to those he finds useful or agreeable to his views and looks to silence those who do not please him. Making a pitch for censorship, Jack declares, "We don't need the conch any more. We know who ought to say things. What good did Simon do speaking?"

Yet Simon is the only boy who has insight into the nature of the true beast, the abstraction that Jack feels watching him in the jungle. Pondering all the characteristics of this animal beast Samneric seem to have discovered, Simon sees that all the pieces don't add up: If this beast had claws and wings, why was it not fast or fierce enough to catch Samneric? When Simon tries to visualize what this beast might look like, "there arose before his inward sight the picture of a human at once heroic and sick" which is a depiction of Golding's vision of humanity as flawed by inherent evil. Golding gives this knowledge to Simon, an outsider, to reflect the place visionaries or mystics typically hold in soci-ety: on the fringes, little understood by the majority, and so often feared or disregarded. As a mystic, Simon is not fully present in the physical world, living so inside his head that he can't keep from banging it into a tree as they make their way to the castle rock. Simon was unable the night before to make the other boys see his outlook; even Ralph, with his new appreciation for thought and wisdom, dismisses Simon without considering that he may have valuable insight.

Character Insight

Ralph has more pressing concerns in light of this crisis. As the leader, he feels the obligation to lead the way into the unexplored territory at the castle rock, even though he is initially as frightened as everyone else. He even suggests that Jack go first, perhaps daring Jack to live up to his declaration that this is "a hunter's job." Yet Ralph is unable to overlook his own pressing sense of responsibility and takes the lead alone around the cliff. In a credit to the conditioning he received back home, politeness is his default even in this tense moment. As he is about to embark, Simon mumbles, perhaps in an attempt to comfort him, that he doesn't believe in the beast; Ralph "answered him politely, as if agreeing about the weather. 'No. I suppose not.'" British culture is famed for such civilized reserve in emotional times; by the standards of the society he's left behind, Ralph is a gentleman. The calmness of his reply is also a testament to his strong alliance with reason, further characterizing Ralph as person who values thought and logic.

When Ralph is actually on the path, he "realized with surprise that he did not really expect to meet any beast and didn't know what he would do about it if he did." This realization underscores Ralph's ability to remain calm and realistic in stressful situations. During the showdown with Jack during the morning's assembly, his clearheaded response helped him maintain his authority; the boys found his hope for rescue during this height of fear more appealing than Jack's desire to hunt. Jack self-indulgently seeks the glory of the hunt while Ralph seeks safety for the group, a fact not lost on the other boys at the time.

Inevitably, once Ralph has accepted the obligation that comes with leadership and has made his way alone toward the castle rock, Jack follows. "Couldn't let you do it on your own," he explains, motivated less by concern than by an inability to allow Ralph his full share of glory as a solo explorer. Immediately, Jack claims the area as ideal for a fort and identifies a loose boulder as a weapon. The other boys warm up to Jack's plan right away and prefer to remain there playing fort and feeling secure rather than follow Ralph's command that they all make the journey to the fire site to re-light the fire.

The group's favor swings back and forth from Ralph to Jack ever more rapidly. After the successful hunt led by the swaggering Jack, Ralph in contrast has begun to seem to the boys like the absurd, stodgy authority figures back home. Samneric mock his justifiable anger later when they are out of its reach. "Eric sniggered. 'Wasn't he waxy?' . . . 'Remember old Waxy at school?'" Imitating the schoolmaster they had nicknamed Waxy for consistently waxing angry at his students' classroom antics, Samneric laugh at Ralph as well, despite the fact that their desertion of duty caused his anger and the loss of possible rescue. Perhaps they laugh to dispel their guilt or because their childish perspective has already allowed them to forget the loss they caused. Either way, Ralph's priorities are lost on them.

Theme

In this chapter, even Ralph begins to lose sight of his priorities. When he reminds Jack that they need to keep the signal going, he explains "That's all we've got." In the previous chapter, Ralph uses the same phrase about the rules when Jack challenges their usefulness. The rules represent a certain civility of domestic order, which Ralph was hard pressed to create or maintain prior to this current crisis. Now his focus narrows from civility to survival. The smoke signal is truly all they have because he doubts they can kill or control a beast that can't be tracked; all he can hope for now is rescue. Once inside castle rock, however, the area that becomes Jack's domain, a "strange thing happened in his [Ralph's] head. Something flittered there in front of his mind like a bat's wing, obscuring the idea"—the hope for a return to the ponies and tea time of which he dreams. The figure envisioned by Simon of "a human at once heroic and sick" could be a composite of Ralph and Jack. Now getting worn down by the hardships and incomprehensible fears of primitive life and out of reach of the conditioning of civilization, Ralph is gradually becoming infected by the savagery that is rapidly eating away at Jack's humanity.

Glossary

waxy [Brit. Informal] enraged.

polyp any of various cnidarians, as the sea anemone or hydra, having a mouth fringed with many small, slender tentacles bearing stinging cells at the top of a tubelike body.

plinth a course of brick or stone, often a projecting one, along the base of a wall.

embroil to draw into a conflict or fight; involve in trouble.

diffident lacking self-confidence; timid; shy.

Chapter 7

Summary

On their way back to the mountain, Ralph indulges in a fantasy of cleanliness and grooming. Disheartened by the group's dishevelment and dirt, he spends time staring out at the vastness of the sea and realizing how high the odds are against rescue. Simon joins him and, seemingly reading his mind, prophesies that Ralph will make it back home.

On the way to the mountain, Jack leads a pig hunt in which he gets slightly wounded. Ralph gets his first taste of hunting, striking a boar in the snout with his spear. After the boar gets away, the group begins a mock hunt that gets out of control and hurts the boy acting as the pig. Ralph urges the group back on their way, but the difficult path before them impedes their progress. Simon volunteers to cross the island alone to inform Piggy that the others won't be home until after dark.

By the time they reach the base of the mountain, darkness has fallen. Spurred on by Jack's bravado, Ralph, Jack, and Roger volunteer to continue the search for the beast while the other boys return to the platform. Once they reach the burnt patch, Ralph, tired of Jack's continual mocking, challenges Jack to go on by himself; Jack returns from the mountaintop terrified. Roger and Ralph investigate as well and are equally terrified by the image of the beast: the dead paratrooper appears to be a live ape-like creature that seems to look at them when the breeze catches his parachute. All three boys flee to the platform in the dark.

Commentary

Ralph undergoes significant emotional and psychological development in this chapter. Following his spontaneous participation in a pig hunt, he experiences the exhilarating mixture of emotions—"I hit him! The spear stuck in"—comparable to those that drive Jack and the other hunters and which underlie Jack's credibility with the group. He, then, "sunned himself in their new respect and felt that hunting was good after all." Heretofore, Ralph had failed to recognize this instinct to hunt and kill in himself. Now that he has experienced these emotions, he has gained an appreciation that Jack's perspectives and priorities are present, even if latent, within us all. This one experience communicates more to Ralph about hunting's attractions than all the bickering with Jack before. Ralph's humanity is deteriorating; his savage self has been touched and awakened.

Armed with this understanding, he is able to see Jack "infuriatingly, for the first time," recognizing that he could have potentially used Jack as a resource all this time rather than competing with him. Realizing that their current path is severely hindering their progress to the mountain, he now calls on Jack's knowledge of the island, garnered during his hunting activities, to identify an alternate path. As Jack continues to compete rather than cooperate with him, Ralph realizes that Jack becomes aggressive whenever he is no longer in charge.

As Ralph and Jack continue to compete rather than cooperate, the antipathy that each generates in the other becomes more evident. Jack becomes increasingly aggressive in situations involving Ralph and his leadership. At one point, Ralph calls on the knowledge passed on to him by Piggy and challenges Jack directly by asking him, "Why do you hate me?" He doesn't get an answer from Jack, but the reaction of the other boys is that "something indecent had been said." The boys recognize that Ralph is opening up the floodgates of aggression and dislike, which civilized conventions are intended to control. Nevertheless, as the situation slides increasingly toward confrontation, Ralph, the leader, the symbol of civility and hope, "turned away first."

Character Insight

Throughout this chapter, Ralph displays and surprises himself with his coolness under pressure—despite his participation in the crazed attack on Robert and in contrast to his grief-stricken, emotional loss of control in the last chapter. Again and again, he shows a realistic grasp of their situation only to be jeered at by Jack. Despite his pride in hitting the boar, he understands immediately that boys with "foolish wooden stick[s]" as spears are no match for the large powerful animal. "But he'd do us!" he protests when Jack orders the hunters to follow the boar's flight. Jack follows alone and is wounded for his lack of sense. Later Ralph is shocked to find himself accompanying Jack up the mountain in the dark to search for the beast, but his response does not betray him. The coolness of his reply renders invalid Jack's supremely taunting invitation. Such instinctual calm reflects again the same strength Ralph displayed in the previous chapter when he made sure to take the lead at castle rock. While Jack's aggressive resentment has no room for reason, Ralph is not afraid once they have set off to ask for another volunteer to accompany them or to point out that their journey up the mountain in the dark is foolish.

Despite his coolness, Ralph can't help competing with Jack, much to the bloodthirsty crowd's delight. Hearing Jack issue to Ralph the invitation to join him in the nighttime search for the beast, "the other boys . . . turned back to sample this fresh rub of two spirits in the dark." The boys as a group display a certain lust for conflict, evident not only in their fascinated appraisal of the conflict of Jack and Ralph but also in their frenzied attack on Robert. The game innocently begun by Robert and Ralph is not so much boys at play as the beast at work.

Theme

Note that Golding uses the phrase "overmastering" to describe the urge to inflict pain, evoking the theme developed in Chapter 4 with the littlun Henry's experiments with mastery over the tide pool creatures and the hunters imposing their collective will on the slaughtered pig. Stimulated by this chapter's unsuccessful hunt and Robert's vulnerability at the hands of the crowd, the boys are mastered themselves by a larger force, impulses they can neither understand nor acknowledge. Even the victim, Robert, cannot address directly the forces that were driving the group. He alludes to his narrowly averted fate when he points out that to improve this so-called game that "You want a real pig . . . because you've got to kill him." His initial response, however, is to downplay his justifiable fear and attempt to regain his place within the group by saying "Oh, my bum!" as if a sore bottom were the extent of the damage. Perhaps he realizes on an instinctive level that maintaining his status as one of the group is critical to survival: The next time the boys play this game, the outsider, Simon, dies.

Ralph attempts to defuse the frightening attack in which he has just participated by placing the beating within the context of their civilization's legitimate outlets for aggression. "'Just a game,' said Ralph uneasily. 'I got jolly badly hurt at rugger once.'" Maurice, on the other hand, looks to refine the process, suggesting that they add a drum and a fire to do the dance "properly," although he's not sure of why he feels they need these things. Maurice seems to be speaking out of some primeval urge to recreate the rituals of a tribal sacrifice. While both Robert and Roger point out that they'll need a pig to complete the game, realizing that this game properly ends in death, Jack looks for a human, someone who could dress up as a pig. He too must acknowledge on some level that this game will inevitably have fatal consequences and, like a true dictator, suggests using one of the littluns, the most vulnerable and, in his eyes, the least valuable of the group.

Character Insight

Given Simon's need to solitude, it's not surprising that he volunteers to take Ralph's message to Piggy by crossing the island alone. His loner tendencies make the other boys think he's odd, but, for the reader, Simon's credibility as a mystic is established in this chapter. As if he is reading Ralph's mind, Simon interrupts Ralph's strained, tense regard of the ocean's vastness by telling him, "You'll get back to where you came from." Ralph responds with the opinion all the boys hold of Simon: "You're batty." Simon knows he's right, however, and he repeats his prophecy with emphasis. Note that he uses "you" instead of "we," realizing, perhaps, on some level that he, himself, will not make it back. Consumed by his own concerns, Ralph doesn't question Simon's omission of himself but takes comfort in the express certainty of the other boy's prophecy.

Theme

Ralph seeks comfort throughout this chapter in images of home, indulging in a fantasy of bathing and grooming and a recollection of the peaceful life of ponies, cereal and cream, and children's books he had once known. Ralph's perspective on the island has changed drastically from the first day, when "A kind of glamour was spread over . . . the scene." Now as he looks at the other boys and sees how thoroughly grimy they are, he finds their condition very different from "the spectacular dirt of boys who have fallen into mud," a temporary dirtying probably initiated by some good-natured horseplay and easily remedied by a warm bath. This dirtiness is an outer manifestation of the darkening of the soul—the emergence of the evil within.

Ralph now longs for the comfort of the familiar, but the home he wishes for is a glamorized ideal. He remembers his former life as a place where "Everything was all right; everything was good-humored and friendly." The reader, of course, is aware that back home—the world the boys have left—exactly the same sorts of human weaknesses which dominate the boys are playing out in the form of nuclear war. As Ralph looks out at the ocean and viscerally experiences its size and power, he considers how the other side of the island offers "the shield of the quiet lagoon" and midday mirages to protect them all from the truth of the ocean's vastness. Faced with the reality of the ocean, he feels as though hope for rescue, and by extension for civilization, has become a mirage.

The images of civilization are in his head as are its voices—the same voices that conditioned Roger's aim to miss Henry, for example, and Piggy's, chiding him for being childish and another voice scolding him for being foolish enough to allow Jack to goad him into seeking out a potentially dangerous animal in the dark with only two other boys and spears of wood. In counterpart to the voices of civilization in his head is Jack's voice, a disembodied voice in the dark like the figurative devil on his shoulder: "'If you don't want to go on,' said the voice sarcastically, 'I'll go up by myself.'" By not attributing this challenge directly to Jack, Golding not only indicates the supreme darkness in which the boys are working but also emphasizes the evil that Jack represents. He describes Jack as a "stain in the darkness;" when Jack leaves, "The stain vanished. Another took its place."

The other stain is Roger, the darkened figure who joined them when all the other boys fled to the safety of the beach. Roger has already established himself as mean-spirited, coldly following the littlun Henry to frighten him with stones that just miss. During Robert's beating, Roger was "fighting to get close," to take part in the hurting before it ended. Finally, it is symbolically significant that, in this second ascent up the mountain, Roger, who is evil and sadistic, has replaced Simon, who is spiritual and mystic, representing the devolution of the boys toward their primitive, savage nature. Later chapters reveal Roger as more sadistic even than Jack.

Confronted with the dead paratrooper, however, Roger is just as terrified as the other two boys. They fear the dead man because they believe him to be a live, predatory creature. He is merely a catalyst, however, for the savagery that will run amok on the island. Just as Ralph feels himself taken over by the bloodlust that infects the hunters, he gets a taste of hatred as a means of courage, forcing himself to approach the false beast by fusing "his fear and loathing into a hatred," a hatred that bolsters his will and drives him forward to investigate where his good sense tells him not to go. When this ape-like creature "lifted its head, holding toward them the ruin of a face," it is showing them the ruin of their humanity as their instinctive evil begins to take over when they are weakened by fear.

Glossary

dun dull grayish-brown.

coverts covered or protected places; shelters.

toilet the process of dressing or grooming oneself.

scurfy having a condition, as dandruff, in which the skin sheds little, dry scales.

brine water full of salt.

do us here, kill us.

bum [Brit. Slang] the buttocks.

rugger [Brit. Informal] rugby.

funk a cowering or flinching through fear; panic.

windy long-winded, pompous, boastful.

impervious not affected by something or not feeling the effects of something.

Chapter 8

Summary

Ralph angers Jack by telling Piggy that even Jack would hide if the beast attacked them. In retaliation, Jack attempts his most serious mutiny yet, trying to convince the other boys to impeach Ralph. When the boys refuse to openly vote against Ralph, Jack announces his defection and runs off into the forest.

Simon suggests they all go face whatever's on the mountain, but no one wants to go. Piggy, glad that Jack is gone, suggests they build a signal fire on the beach so that they won't have to go up the mountain. While everyone gathers wood, most of the biguns creep away to join Jack. Simon disappears as well, going to his hidden spot in the forest to rest after his unsuccessful address to the group. Piggy starts the fire with his glasses.

Meanwhile Jack leads another successful hunt, attacking and killing a nursing sow and then impaling her head on a stick as an offering to the beast, coincidentally in full view of the spot where Simon sits concealed. Simon hallucinates, thinking that the head is talking to him, until he loses consciousness.

To get fire for a pig roast, Jack stages a theft of some burning branches from the beach fire and invites Ralph's group to the roast in an attempt to recruit them to join his tribe. Ralph tries to rally his group to his side but loses his train of thought when he tries to remember the importance of being rescued, causing them to doubt him briefly.

Commentary

Ralph speaks realistically when he tells Piggy that even Jack would hide if the beast attacked; after all, the night before Jack had been as terrified as the other two boys when he saw the dead paratrooper. Jack cannot accept this realistic view of himself. In defense, he offers to the group a rationale for impeaching Ralph—"He'd never have got us meat," as if hunting skills make for an effective leader. Noting that "He isn't a prefect and we don't know anything about him" opens up speculation about Ralph's qualifications as a leader.

Jack further condemns Ralph as one who talks rather than one who gets results, but Ralph himself has long ago lost patience with talk, finding it an ineffective and inappropriate tool for their situation. His position on the usefulness of rhetoric is clear in his response to Jack's assembly. "'Talk,' said Ralph bitterly, 'Talk, talk, talk.'"

Reluctant to vote openly against Ralph, the boys sneak off to join Jack and return only when masked by their new tribal war paint, which has a liberating effect. Jack so loses himself in this liberation that, symbolizing the casting off of all social and civil encumbrances, he abandons clothing altogether, wearing only his paint and his knife when he presents his invitation to Ralph's group. "He was safe from shame or self-consciousness behind the mask of his paint."

Character Insight

Jack strives to be a chief in some grand fashion seen in a book or a movie, evidenced by the bizarrely formal announcement and flourish he makes Maurice and Robert perform once he has spoken to Ralph's group. Little does he realize he himself is fulfilling the role of the beast. Wrapped up in the caveman-like activities of hunting, face-painting, and chest-beating disguised as addresses to the assembly, Jack doesn't feel the need for rescue and so distracts the other boys from keeping the fire lit. He tells the assembly "Yes. The beast is a hunter" without taking a moment to reflect that perhaps the hunter is the beast.

Theme

Having lost and been wounded by the powerful, aggressive boar in the previous chapter, Jack chooses now to attack a defenseless sow who is vulnerable while she nurses her piglets—an act of supreme cruelty. The sow's death and disfigurement marks the triumph of evil and the climax of the novel. Jack's selection of the vulnerable sow arises from his defeated attempt to depose Ralph and foreshadows his later actions. While he couldn't impeach Ralph openly and was wounded emotionally in the attempt, he can defeat him by killing the defenseless boys in his tribe, Piggy and Simon.

Voices can be a tool of evil as well. In the previous chapter, Jack's voice came unidentified out of the darkness like the devil's voice. While his choirboys-turned-hunters prepare unknowingly in this chapter to commit cruelty against their former friends and group members by joining Jack, Golding points out for contrast that "their voices had been the song of angels" back in civilization. Now they take part in slaughtering a mother pig and putting her head on a stake, offering it to the supposed beast while "The silence accepted the gift."

Theme

Note that when the sow's head speaks to Simon, it takes on a male voice, becoming the Lord of the Flies. Interestingly, Piggy and the Lord of the Flies both give the same answer to the same question, although they each phrase it slightly differently. Ralph asks Piggy "what makes things break up like they do?" and receives the reply "I dunno. I expect it's him . . . Jack." Meanwhile Simon hears the staked head tell him, "You knew, didn't you? . . . I'm the reason why it's no go? Why things are what they are?" The Lord of the Flies, a literal translation of the Greek word Beelzebub, symbolizes evil, and Jack is evil personified. Piggy's assessment of the problem is actually much tamer in intent, based not on a consideration of evil but what he terms a lack of common sense (reason).

True to Piggy's assertion that "It's them that haven't no common sense that make trouble on this island," Jack doesn't seem to have much common sense. He dictates to his hunters that they forget the beast and stop having nightmares, as if either mental process could be controlled on command. Piggy has a more rational solution to their situation, one that actually requires more courage on the boys' part than Jack's foolishly unrealistic demands. "We just got to go on, that's all. That's what grownups would do." Ralph wishes he could think more like a grownup, impressed with Piggy's astuteness in noting that Samneric need to take separate shifts in tending the fire rather than taking their turn together. Piggy and Ralph rely on adult behavior as a model because they still maintain the image of grownups as eminently capable and reasonable. They equate adulthood with knowledge and higher understanding.

In a way, Simon shares the same perception but sees the darker side of knowledge. He sees the sow's eyes as "dim with the infinite cynicism of adult life" and later hears the head speak with a schoolmaster's voice, telling him to accept the presence of evil on the island. This view of adults is not defined by the civilized politeness and capability the boys imagined just two nights before, after the assembly. Cynicism results from gaining experience while losing optimism; having witnessed the pig's slaughter and defacement has given Simon experience in death and brutality and caused him to lose hope. Yet he soldiers on in his quest to discover the identity of the beast on the mountain top, the beast he knows is false because he has just had a conversation with the true beast.

Just as Piggy and Simon seem to share an idea about the cause of the island society's disintegration, Simon and Jack have similar revelations as well. During the first successful hunt in Chapter 4, Jack is excited by "the knowledge that had come to them when they closed in on the struggling pig." In this chapter, Simon's "gaze was held by that ancient, inescapable recognition" as he looks upon the Lord of the Flies. Both boys are connecting with the savagery that begets evil, but Jack revels in it while Simon is undone by it, trapped by his vision of the Lord of the Flies in his hidden spot until he passes out.

Another concept related to this knowledge of savagery is a twist on the idea of fun. From the beginning, Ralph's goal for the group was for everyone to have fun. Such a goal did not seem farfetched given that the boys were on a pristine tropical island, the type featured in the adventure stories they all had read. Once Jack defects and lures his hunters away, he also promises fun, the kind that comes with dressing up like savages and having adventurous hunts. Although Jack may not realize the fun he is promising will turn into deadly cruelty, Simon knows that Jack holding a position of power can have only ill effects for the more vulnerable boys like Piggy, the littluns, and himself. Simon hears the Lord of the Flies say, "We're going to have fun on this island! So don't try it on . . . or else." Now the offer to have fun is a threat, with the Lord of the Flies warning Simon not to try stopping the consequences of Jack's new regime but to accept the savagery that will overtake the island.

Ralph responds to the defection of the hunters with increasing despair. Wishing he could think more like an adult, he turns to Piggy for advice and insight. Piggy keeps alive the fire when he has the "intellectual daring" to suggest maintaining a fire on the beach instead of on the mountain. During the small assembly held after rebuilding the fire, Piggy prompts Ralph when he forgets what he was going to say. By reminding him of rescue and thinking to move the fire, Piggy is fighting for his survival with his intellect just as Jack looks to conquer with physicality. In the end, Ralph will have to combine both physical abilities and brains to outrun Jack's tribe. For now, Ralph relies on Piggy for hope and for answers.

Character Insight

Earlier, Simon asked the boys a question so fundamental that they couldn't answer it: "What else is there to do?" In a way, the boys spend the rest of the book responding to this question but never in the way Simon wants them to. He sees the need to face their fears, to approach the beast on the mountain in daylight in order to understand its true identity and get on with the business of facing the beast within themselves. Instead, the others respond with various avoidance methods:

Jack offering a libation, a head on a stake, Ralph moving the fire to the beach, Piggy advocating a pragmatic perseverance. Their responses are indicative of each boy's character: Jack focuses on the concrete action of a primitive offering, Ralph wants to keep the home fire burning, and Piggy remains devoted to logic and realism.

Glossary

prefect in some private schools, esp. in England, an older student with disciplinary authority.

rebuke to blame or scold in a sharp way; reprimand.

cracked [Informal] mentally unbalanced; crazy.

Chapter 9

Summary

As a storm builds over the island, Simon awakens from his faint and makes his way to the beast sighting on the mountain. He finds the paratrooper's body, inspects it, and realizes its true identity. From his vantage point, he can see that most of the boys are at the fire at Jack's camp, so he heads there to give everyone the news. He is so weakened by the day's experiences that he can barely walk.

Ralph and Piggy realize even the biguns loyal to Ralph have gone to Jack's party. They go as well, out of curiosity and hunger. Jack allows them to eat but, when everyone is finished eating, calls for all the boys to indicate whether they'd like to join his group or remain with Ralph's. Ralph makes a pitch for the boys to stay with him, reminding them of the first day's election. Jack has a strong hold on them, however, playing up the role of tribal chief.

The storm breaks over the party. Jack orders a dance in response to the downpour. Ralph and Piggy join in the outer fringes of the dance as well. Suddenly, Simon crawls out of the forest and into the center of the dance circle. He tries to tell them about the true identity of the beast sighted on the mountain but can barely make himself heard over the storm and the boys' now frenzied chanting. Overcome by its own momentum, the group turns on Simon as if he were the beast and kills him. The rain increases and the boys back off, leaving Simon's body on the beach. That night, the tide carries his body away.

The storm's wind fills the dead soldier's parachute and lifts him up and over the island and out to sea. This sight terrifies the boys, and they scatter, screaming.

Commentary

This chapter focuses on Simon and the fulfillment of his role as a visionary mystic. Awakening from his faint, he asks again out loud the question he put to the assembly in the previous chapter: "What else is there to do?" He must face whatever is on the mountain. That confrontation seems to have aged him: he walks with the difficulty of an old man, as if bowed down by "the infinite cynicism of adult life" that he saw in the pig's eyes.

Simon doesn't seem to fear the beast sighted on the mountain. Given the doubts he had in Chapter 6 about this supposed beast and having had a visitation from the true beast, the Lord of the Flies, Simon has moved past fear into another arena of emotion. Approaching the frightful figure on the mountain, he sees it sit up and look at him; in response "He hid his face" as if in shame over the boys' misconceptions about its menace. Then he frees the lines of the soldier's parachute from the rocks, enabling the dead soldier to fly off during the storm, which it does upon Simon's death.

In a way, the soldier is actually working as an agent of the true beast, bringing out the worst in the boys. They do not band together to overcome this fearful situation but allow their own worst impulses to surface and dominate, fragmenting into opposing groups and killing one of their own in a frenzy of fear and savagery. Considering that his arrival on the island was brought about by a battle of the ongoing war, the soldier truly was an emissary of the beast, the savagery that lurks in humanity.

Of the boys, only Simon took the presence of an unidentified creature on the mountain as a sign to be explored or a symbol to be considered, rather than as an indication of an animal-beast's presence. By courageously seeking out the figure on the mountain, Simon fulfills his destiny of revelation. Having confronted both the Lord of the Flies (the sow's head on a stick) and the so-called beast (the soldier's corpse), Simon understands the nature of the evil on the island. He doesn't get to share his revelation with the other boys because they are not ready to accept or understand it. They are living out the true beast's actions while they think of themselves as playacting the roles of painted savages, which is Jack's idea of fun—and the true beast's as well.

When the tide carries off Simon's body, covered in the jellyfish-like phosphorescent creatures that come in with the tide, Golding shifts the focus from Simon's body's movements to the much larger progressions of the sun, moon, and earth because Simon represents a knowledge as fundamental as the elements.

Golding uses the weather to symbolize a kind of universal assessment of the actions that have taken place in the novel and as a way to underscore the tension between and extreme reactions of the boys. He opens the chapter with an ominous description of the odd weather over the island: "the air was ready to explode . . . a brassy glare had taken the place of clear daylight." Then the downpour starts in earnest immediately after Simon's death, as though the weather were responding to the boys' actions. The use of the weather as a dramatic technique is an ancient and effective tool.

The desire for drama underlies the other boys' desertion, Ralph tells Piggy. He assesses accurately their basic motivation not as a wish to do evil but for the drama and game of Jack's primal theater. They are also drawn in by the enticement of meat and the protection that Jack seems to provide as a fearless, aggressive hunter. Jack certainly is taken with the drama of it, forcing the other boys to perform the bizarrely formal rituals. This role is no game for him though; by the time Ralph and Piggy reach the party, Jack has clearly gone power-mad. Evoking images of Kurtz from Joseph Conrad's *Heart of Darkness*, Jack sits on a large log, "painted and garlanded . . . like an idol." Around him are arranged piles of food and drink as though they are offerings to him.

Just as Jack and the dead soldier seemed to have in common a desire to keep the fire from being lit, they now have in common a link with apes. Ralph saw the dead soldier as "something like a great ape" hunched over—a connection between the animality of the apes from which humans are descended and the animality still present in humankind today. Now as Jack sits in front of his tribe and considers the new arrivals, Ralph and Piggy, "Power . . . chattered in his ear like an ape." The devil on his shoulder is his own animality, looking to master other creatures. He already has achieved mastery of those of his tribe: When he commands that someone bring him a drink, someone does. They also address him as "Chief," a formality not demanded by Ralph. Jack expects subservience from his tribe, which they accept as though he can protect them through strength of personality alone. Ralph is unable to enforce his rules or his authority because he lacks Jack's punitive nature and relies instead on the boys' sense of honor in following through on their promises.

When the rain starts, Jack orders the boys to dance in the rain, playing out the same mock hunt in which Robert was hurt. The dance gives order to the boys' panicked energy during the downpour and acts as a defiance of the elements, a sort of rain dance in reverse. Even Ralph and Piggy decide not to run immediately for the shelters but instead join in on the fringes. In this situation, they find themselves seeking a more abstract kind of shelter instead in "this demented but partly secure society" wherein "the brown backs of the fence . . . hemmed in the terror and made it governable."

The sense of protection in the repetitive chanting and the circular movements of the dance provides the boys with another strong motivation for staying with Jack, a motivation Ralph hadn't considered when he commented to Piggy that the biguns joined Jack to play like savages with the hunting and face paint. Jack has tapped into the power of repetitive rituals, where the person performing the ritual feels "as though repetition would achieve safety of itself" despite the circumstances. Repetitive rituals are present in nearly every cohesive group, from churchgoers performing the same prayers and rites every Sunday to political parties chanting their slogans to military personnel following their prescribed daily routines. Repetition provides comfort for the group because all the individual members know what is expected of them within the context of the ritual and, by extension, within the group.

Being part of Jack's tribe, with its attendant rituals and subservience, allows the boys to feel as though they are relieved of all responsibility for what happens during their ritual dance. While some of the boys, such as Ralph, felt uneasy with the beating Robert received in Chapter 7, other boys simply enjoyed the "game" and thought of ways to refine it, such as Maurice suggesting they add drums. Yet they all participated, drawn in by their animal selves. In this chapter, the same effect is aggravated by the intensity of the thunder and the darkness.

Golding describes the mob murder scene: "There were no words and no movements but the tearing of teeth and claws." Again savagery is connected with a lack of verbal communication; language is, of course, one of humankind's greatest inventions and that which separates humanity most dramatically from the lower forms of creatures. Further, Golding uses the phrase "teeth and claws" (representing the primitive use of physical attributes or features as weapons) instead of spears (the use of tools as weapons). The phrase also recalls Samneric's fanciful description of the beast as having teeth and claws (although they neither felt nor saw them in reality). In this instance, the true beast—evil —acts through the frenzied mob; those imagined teeth and claws bare themselves for real.

Once the frenzy dies down, however, the boys back off their prey and are astonished to see "how small a beast it was." The truth of what they have done begins filtering in. Their responses to the act they have committed are explored in Chapter 10.

Glossary

derision contempt or ridicule.

phosphorescence a continuing luminescence without noticeable heat.

Chapter 10

Summary

The next morning, Ralph finds that only Piggy, Samneric, and some littluns remain in his camp. Brooding over the previous night's events, he points out to Piggy that they murdered Simon. Piggy objects to the use of the term "murder" and doesn't want Samneric to know that he and Ralph were at least somewhat involved in the deadly dance. Samneric don't want to admit their own involvement, either.

Jack begins acting ever more like a cruel dictator to his own tribe members, having one of the boys tied up and beaten for angering him. He plans a raid on Ralph's camp to get fire for another pig roast and tries to convince his uneasy followers that they had beaten but not killed the beast the previous night. The beast had come to them in disguise, he asserts, in utter denial that they had killed one of their former group.

Back at Ralph's camp, the boys decide to let the fire die for the night rather than collect more wood in the dark. Because Jack and his raiders can't steal burning branches, they attack Ralph's group and steal Piggy's glasses.

Commentary

Character Insight

This chapter reveals the boys' responses to their actions of the night before, when they beat Simon to death in a tribal frenzy. Ralph is the only character who names the deed as murder and has a realistic, unvarnished view of his participation. Back at the platform, he takes a seat in front of the chief's log rather than on it and contemplates the horror of what they've done. He feels both loathing and excitement over the kill he witnessed, as Jack experienced the first time he killed a pig. He shudders at Piggy's touch on his shoulder; humanity has let him down. Putting the pieces together, he recalls the parachuted figure drifting off the night before and Simon's shouting about a dead man on the mountain, musing that the life-like figure they saw on the mountaintop might have been the dead paratrooper rather than an actual animal-beast. Getting to the heart of the matter, he says, "I'm frightened. Of us."

Although he initially owns up to his active role in the fatal dance, as a defense mechanism, Ralph willingly takes the opportunity Piggy gives him to deny full participation, entering into a sort of functional denial. When Piggy reminds Ralph that he himself remained on the outside of the circle, Ralph tries to amend his position as well, now claiming that he, too, was on the outside of the circle and so could not have done as much damage as the boys in the inner ring.

Piggy is in full-fledged denial of anyone's responsibility, unable to process the death without blaming Simon for his seemingly odd behavior. Ever the pragmatist, Piggy complains, "What good're you doing talking like that?" when Ralph brings up the highly charged issue of Simon's death at their hands. True, his involvement is somewhat limited; as Ralph mentions, Piggy stayed on the outside of the circle. Golding doesn't provide a reason as to why Piggy remained on the outside, whether his position was due to his physical inability to make his way into the inner circle or whether he simply wasn't able to tap into the animality of the more physically abled boys or both. Golding, however, does include Piggy in the damning description of the boys as they sit on the platform that morning, with the sun shining on their "befouled bodies."

Piggy tries to keep life scientific and intellectual, despite the previous night's emotionally charged incident, "searching for a formula" to explain the death. He asserts that the assault on Simon was justifiable because Simon asked for it by inexplicably crawling out of the forest into the ring. Piggy, of course, is unaware that Simon had to crawl because his visionary confrontation with the true beast had so weakened him.

In responding to the death, Jack takes an entirely different direction from logic or common sense, in direct conflict with the actual events they had all witnessed. Perhaps acting out of some guilt he is unable to acknowledge, Jack becomes paranoid, posting guards at the entrance to the castle rock area in case any of Ralph's tribe tries to enter. One of the boys questions this concern and Jack replies, "They'll try to spoil things we do." Ironically, he is also taking the part of the true beast, the Lord of the Flies, who told Simon not to try and stop the "fun" that was going to take place on the island.

The entrance guards serve another purpose as well—to protect the tribe from the beast. Jack tells his tribe that they did not, in fact, kill the beast, just beat it as it came in disguise. Therefore, they still need to appease it and be on the alert. He prescribes their reality now as he had dictated their dreams and emotions in the previous chapter. This technique for truth control is standard in tyrannical regimes. Because none of the boys want to admit their participation in the "obscene" dance, they allow Jack to dictate their reality. They find comfort in his overbearing authority, as if he can protect them from their indefinable fears through strength of his personality alone. More concretely, Jack offers them the protection of weaponry and an instinct for warfare. When Roger sees the boulder that stands ready to crush interlopers at the entrance to Castle Rock, he deems Jack "a proper chief" because he's got weaponry, the makings of war.

Character Insight

For a sadist like Roger, joining the tribe offers him the chance to unleash his cruelty amidst Jack's reign of "irresponsible authority." All his life, Roger has been conditioned to leash or mask his impulses, as evidenced by his inability to actually hit Henry with the stones in Chapter 4. Hearing that Jack has had Wilfred arbitrarily bound and left to wait hours for punishment strikes a responsive chord in Roger. By the end of the next chapter, he carves out a distinct niche in the tribe as the hangman, the torturer who plays a key role in all dictatorships.

Jack doesn't consider himself "a chief . . . in truth" until he accomplishes the theft of Piggy's glasses. In this way, Jack symbolizes a twisted Prometheus, stealing fire from the humans to profit the savages as opposed to stealing from the gods to benefit humans. Note that originally he and his group of choirboys were to play the role of Prometheus in maintaining the fire, maintaining a visual plea to civilization for rescue and quick return home.

Ralph's connection with his civilized self fades even more rapidly now, although he fights to maintain it and is baffled by the "curtain" that seems to fall when he tries to stress the importance of the fire. When the twins question the value of keeping the fire lit, Ralph "tried indignantly to remember. There was something good about a fire." Piggy, of course, instantly knows what this good is, as his connection to civilization remains very strong because it offers him protection that is lacking on the island.

Piggy is so intent on preserving some remnant of civilization on the island that he not only remains loyal to Ralph but to the concept of civilized discourse represented by the conch. He assumes, improbably enough, that Jack's raiders have attacked them to get the conch. Just as he takes for granted that Ralph has not lost his focus on rescue and home, he figures that Jack still places a value on what the conch represents when obviously Jack has abandoned all that, preferring the life of savagery. Jack's leadership is based on fear; he has abandoned the conch for the dance.

The loss of his glasses to the savages literally renders Piggy more helpless and ineffectual and symbolically deprives Ralph of his intellectual counselor. The alert reader understands that Piggy will be the next victim.

Glossary

gesticulate to make or use gestures, esp. with the hands and arms, as in adding nuances or force to one's speech, or as a substitute for speech.

torrid so hot as to be parching or oppressive; scorching.

Reds [Slang] Communists.

lamp standard lamppost.

barmy [Brit. Slang] crazy.

round the bend [Brit. Informal] crazy; insane.

bomb happy [Slang, Chiefly Brit.] crazy; insane.

crackers [Slang, Chiefly Brit.] crazy; insane.

pills [Vulgar Brit Slang] the testicles.

bowstave here, slightly curved arc like that of a bow.

Chapter 11

Summary

Ralph calls an assembly at Piggy's urging, wherein they decide the four remaining biguns will ask Jack's tribe for the glasses back, reminding them of a signal fire's importance. Samneric express a real fear of approaching the other boys who have now become complete savages.

Jack's tribe is hostile to Ralph's little group; Roger throws stones at the twins to scare them. Jack emerges from the forest where he had been hunting and tells Ralph to go back to his end of the island. When Ralph calls him a thief for stealing Piggy's glasses, they fence briefly with their spears before Piggy reminds Ralph to focus on their agenda.

The savages laugh derisively at Ralph's impassioned speech about the necessity of a signal fire. Then Jack orders his tribe to grab Samneric and tie them up, prompting a fistfight between himself and Ralph. Again, Piggy interrupts and, holding the conch, attempts a speech as well. While Piggy admonishes the boys for becoming savages, Roger releases a huge boulder in Piggy's direction, knocking him off the cliff to his death on the rocks below. A large wave quickly carries off his body.

Jack screams in victory at Ralph and then throws his spear at him. The spear wounds Ralph but bounces off, and Ralph flees for his life. Samneric remain tied up in the hands of the savages, menaced by Jack and soon to be tortured by Roger.

Commentary

As the last three biguns remaining with Ralph, they have a great stake in quickly developing some solutions to Piggy's virtual blindness and the loss of a signal fire, as well as protecting themselves from Jack's deadly tribe. Piggy insists that Ralph call an assembly to discuss the matter. Although blowing the conch to summon only themselves seems rather ridiculous, Piggy asserts that "It's the only thing we got." Assemblies regulated by the conch still bring him comfort despite their lack of effectiveness.

In fact, the conch is the only tool of authority or action left to them, but it's an ineffectual one, given the savages' loss of regard for it. When Ralph blows the conch at Castle Rock, for example, the savages greet him with silence and a stone thrown at Sam by Roger. The conch symbolizes not only the power *to* speak during assembly but also the power *of* speech itself, an ability that separates humans from animals. In a way, the savages cause Ralph to lose his power of speech, when he gives up his address on the importance of rescue because he is "defeated by the silence and the painted anonymity." With the exceptions of Jack's commands, the savages' reactions to Ralph's and Piggy's speeches are all non-verbal: jeering, laughing, booing, and a general "clamor." Following Roger's impulsive assassination of Piggy, "the silence was complete" as Piggy provided the last bastion of human intellect and reason on the island.

Even up to the moment of his death, Piggy's perspective doesn't shift in response to the reality of their situation. At their little assembly, he demands action, still relying on Ralph to get things done despite the obvious disregard for his authority shown by all of Jack's tribe. Piggy cannot think as the others think or value what they value. Because his eminently sensible approach to life is modeled on the attitudes and rules of the authoritative adult world, he thinks everyone should share his values and attitudes as a matter of course. Speaking of the deaths of Simon and the littlun with the birthmark who had first brought up the beast as a concern, he asks "What's grownups goin' to think?" as if he is not so much mourning the boys' deaths as he is mourning the loss of values, ethics, discipline, and decorum that caused those deaths. Claiming that Jack has "got to" return his glasses because "what's right's right," he reveals that he holds a certain code of ethics to be universal and non-negotiable, as fundamental as fire. In reality ethics originate from a particular society's values and expectations; Jack's subculture has radically different ethics from Ralph's.

Samneric fully appreciate this difference; their change in perspective is evident at the assembly. In Chapter 6, they speak mockingly of a schoolmaster nicknamed Old Waxy as if his waxing anger was nothing to fear. Now they fear for their lives, saying that if Jack "gets waxy we've had it." Even more devastating to their morale is Ralph's oddly timed outburst of "smoke! We've got to have smoke." From his delivery, they realize Ralph can't remember why they need smoke but is just mouthing the words as a sort of desperate plea for clarity. Piggy, too, grasps that Ralph has forgotten the purpose of smoke; his reminder of smoke's purpose makes Ralph defensive. Ralph's denial of his fallibility causes them to view him as fallible. They look at him as though "seeing him for the first time": a boy trying to accomplish what an adult would have difficulty achieving in these circumstances—reasoning with a pack of killers.

Character Insight

Roger, the sadist, relishes the role of a killer. In Chapter 4, Roger is restrained from throwing stones directly at other boys by the social discipline internalized during his former life. When he makes Sam nearly lose his footing with a well-placed stone throw, Roger experiences viscerally the mastery he can now wield over others, and the reader recognizes a dramatic change. Like Samneric, Roger's perspective has changed with the power shift on the island. From his point of view on top of Castle Rock, "Ralph was a shock of hair and Piggy a bag of fat"; they are not humans or other boys to him. Mentally dehumanizing those not in his group frees Roger from the restraints of decency, an effect he feels as "a sense of delirious abandonment" when he releases the rock that kills Piggy.

Theme

Perceiving other humans as less than human is the basis of an infinite number of prejudices and bigotry as well as the moral underpinning of genocide. Jack's boys enthusiastically bind Samneric because they sense Samneric's "otherness"; that otherness allows the savages to justify their cruelty against their own kind. Such a mental adjustment is also necessary for soldiers to make in order to justify killing their enemies who are part of the family of humanity, an adjustment made even by the very civil and polite naval officer who ultimately rescues the boys. All the boys made that adjustment themselves when they chose to perceive Simon as the beast rather than as one of their own.

Although all the boys were guilty in Simon's death, the other savages perceive Roger differently after Piggy's death. Because he calmly and single-handedly kills someone, he is marked as a hangman, one who "wields a nameless authority." Just as Ralph has an instinct for diplomacy and leadership, Roger has an instinct for torture. Without the "protection of parents and school and policeman and the law" which surrounded Henry in Chapter 4 and forced Roger to miss when he threw stones, Roger is free within Jack's primitive subculture to make deadly contact.

Ralph seeks to remind the savages of those very constraints, to summon the conditioning voices of civilization that always warned them to play nice and share with others. At the assembly, he suggests that his group present an image of their former, civilized selves when approaching the savages. He wants to differentiate his group from Jack's tribe, as if to remind them of what they've lost or tantalize them with what they could have if rescue is achieved. In contrast, Samneric want to put on paint, hoping for mercy through assimilation. They fear that reminding Jack of the constraints he's now free of will only aggravate his abuse of power. "They'll be painted! You know how it is." Sadly, the twins turn out to be correct about the antagonizing effect of "otherness." When Jack orders his boys to bind the twins, Samneric "protested out of the heart of civilization" with language that marks them as outsiders in this group, which has left behind such civilized verbal niceties as "Oh, I say!"

Style & Language

Seeing the twins bound, Ralph's language gets to the heart of the matter quickly. He shouts at Jack, calling him "a beast and a swine and a bloody, bloody thief!" This emotional accusation is in fact truthful. Jack is living out the beast's urges, the beast that spoke to Simon in the guise of a swine head. Jack stole not only Piggy's glasses, but also hope, rescue, Simon's life, Ralph's authority, and the vestiges of civilization from their small island culture. Ralph's use of "bloody" works not only as an expletive but also as an accurate adjective, considering the deaths Jack has caused by fostering an environment of enmity coupled with ferocity.

Initially, Jack and Ralph feel some reluctance to engage fully in combat. When Ralph calls him a thief, Jack rushes at Ralph threateningly with his spear, but they each wield their spears more like sabers, unwilling to use the "the lethal points." They verbally square off, daring each other to come fight but remaining out of each other's reach. Up to this point, none of the boys have fought to the death one on one. Simon's death occurred in the midst of a group frenzy. Even Roger does not engage in hand-to-hand combat but acts more as a physically removed assassin. Until Jack acts after Piggy's death and flings his spear dead-on at Ralph, he is no doubt at some level reluctant to kill another boy for the same reason he couldn't kill the first piglet he encountered in Chapter 1: "because of the enormity of the knife descending and cutting into living flesh."

Theme

In addition, Ralph and Jack are connected through a love/hate relationship that neither one of them understands, a link Ralph thinks of as "an indefinable connection" in Chapter 12. They began on the first day with the glamour of a new friendship; "They were lifted up: were friends." Golding's use of the phrase "lifted up" to describe their friendship implies that a partnership between the humane and the bestial components of humanity can result in great things. Yet the two forces must remain in balance to produce positive effects. The conflict on this island begins with Jack attempting to dominate the group rather than work with Ralph to benefit it. For his part, Ralph remains so focused on promoting a sense of order that he overlooks the boys' desire for food more substantial than fruit. Because Ralph so strongly identifies with the civilized part of himself, he cannot understand how Jack can live so far within his animal side. Once Jack makes an attempt on Ralph's life, however, appreciation for each other's perspectives is rendered moot as Ralph becomes re-classified as prey rather than as another human being.

Evil has triumphed: Spirituality, creativity, and religion went with the demise of Simon; intellect and reason die with Piggy; and rules, authority, and tradition are destroyed with the conch.

Glossary

myopia nearsightedness.

propititate win or regain the good will of; appease or conciliate.

pinnacles pointed formations; peaks, as at the tops of mountains.

pinch [Slang] to steal.

truculent fierce; cruel; savage; ferocious.

talisman anything thought to have magic power; a charm.

Chapter 12

Summary

While the tribe feasts inside Castle Rock, Ralph makes his way back to the platform. Once there, he is reluctant to spend the night alone in the shelter and decides to return to Jack's end of the island to try reasoning with them again. On the way, he encounters the pig's skull that had spoken to Simon. Finding it eerily life-like and knowing, he knocks it to the ground and takes the stake as a weapon.

Back at Castle Rock, he sees that Samneric are on watch, having been forced to join the tribe. He approaches them cautiously, hoping to win back their loyalty. They tell him of the manhunt planned for the next day and give him some meat. Someone from the tribe hears them talking to Ralph and punishes them.

Ralph finds a place to sleep for the night. The next morning, his hiding place, a dense thicket, is betrayed by Samneric. The tribe is unsuccessful at reaching him in the thicket, so they flush him out by rolling boulders into it and setting it on fire. Once Ralph is on the run, the tribe follows him, communicating with each other with an ululating cry.

Ralph finds another impenetrable thicket to hide in but is discovered there as well. Now the fire has spread across the island so that he has to outrun the savages and the fire. He makes it to the beach and falls at the feet of a newly arrived British naval officer, whose ship had been attracted by the smoke from the huge fire. The officer confirms that his ship will take them off the island. Ralph breaks into sobs, weeping for all he has lost.

Commentary

Watching the savages retreat, Ralph tries to identify them as individuals and guesses one to be Bill. Then he realizes that, in fact, "this was not Bill" and he's right: Once divorced from his previously civilized self in appearance, behavior, and values, the individual who was Bill is gone. In the previous chapter, after Jack throws a spear with deadly intention at Ralph, Golding stops using Jack's name and refers to him as "the chief." The boy named Jack has been totally replaced with a primal entity, the personification of the beast's lust for power and the rejection of the civilizing forces represented by Ralph.

Even after the attack, Ralph so craves human companionship—the devil he knows—that he returns to Castle Rock to reason with Jack's tribe again on the next day, relying on their "daylight sanity." "Daylight sanity" is another term for common sense; Piggy tells Ralph in Chapter 8 that lack of common sense is the source of all the trouble on the island. At the time, Piggy referred to practicality, or a sound judgement of the actions they would need to take to attract a rescue ship and coexist with some amount of civility.

Common sense could also be understood, however, as communal sentiment, a shared sensibility of what's important and what's allowed. Ralph "knew he was an outcast. 'Cos I had some sense,'" he tells himself—not just common sense but a sense of his identity as a civilized person, a sense of the particular morality that had governed the boys' culture back home. When Jack threw the spear at Ralph, Jack made him an outcast, disallowing his easy assimilation into the group even if he had wanted to forsake rescue in favor of hunting. When Ralph tries to reason with the newly tribal twins and gain an understanding of Jack's hatred of him, Eric says "Never mind what's sense. That's gone." Jack's tribe lacks sense in terms of logically justifiable attitudes and behaviors.

In response to his desperate situation, bereft of any companion and the conch as well, Ralph reverts to a childish state. He "whimpered and yawned like a littlun" when facing the coming night with its attendant fears. Later, as he is hunted, he reverts back not in time but in character to his primal self, squatting in a thicket, baring his teeth, and snarling. Becoming the prey brings out the animal survival instincts coupled with innate human intellect in him: He seeks a "lair" in which to spend the night and thinks ahead to his hiding place the next day. He prepares himself to poke whoever discovers him with his spear so that the manhunter "would be stuck, squealing like a pig." Acting purely out of the fundamental drive for survival, he attacks two savages who stand between him and escape, and wounds a third from his hiding place. The members of Jack's tribe have ceased to be human for him; he thinks of them as "those striped and inimical creatures."

Hunting has become their identity rather than their activity. In contrast, Ralph still thinks sensibly even when on the run: when the forest fire burns the fruit trees, he curses the tribe for failing to think ahead when they set the fire: "Fools! . . . what would they eat tomorrow?"

During his flight, Ralph longs for Piggy's counsel, wishing for the solemnity of the assemblies made dignified by the conch rather than having to make life or death decisions while on the run for his life. "If only one had time to think!" he laments. Civilization makes for plenty of time to think, providing institutions like universities where the scholars can devote themselves to mental activities. Such protection allows the abstract arts such as philosophy and theoretical work in the arts and sciences to flourish; in such a protected environment, a fragile boy like Simon could have learned to express fully and accurately his intuitive understanding of humanity's dark side. Note that Simon's prophecy comes back to Ralph in a flash during the hunt. In a moment of great desperation, cornered in his hiding place by a savage and having just realized the purpose of a stick sharpened at both ends, the phrase "You'll get back" surfaces, as if Simon's spirit haunts the island.

If Simon's ghost is present, it is there to comfort Ralph and reach out to him with its knowledge, unlike the Lord of the Flies. When Ralph encounters the Lord of the Flies, he finds a "skull that gleamed as white as ever the conch had done." This description symbolizes the universal and infinite struggle between good and evil. The skull is vested with the knowledge that was revealed to Simon: Evil is present in us all, and we must struggle not to allow it to dominate us.

Knocking the skull to the ground and breaking it into pieces is a small victory over the beast for Ralph. More to the point, he takes the stake on which the head rested so that he has his own stick sharpened at both ends. Like a blade that cuts both ways, he'll use the savage's stick to defend himself from them. Preoccupied with keeping on the move, he doesn't realize until late in the hunt that he is himself carrying a stick sharpened on both ends. At this point he realizes that his head is meant to become the ultimate offering to the beast, the beast's greatest victory yet on the island.

The officer of the gunboat that Ralph encounters simultaneously represents Ralph's original moral naiveté and Jack's propensity toward evil and destruction. As Ralph encounters the officer, he sees not a face but all the markings of the officer's "tribe": the cap with the crown, anchor and gold leaves, the uniform with epaulettes and buttons, and the revolver. The decorative elements of his uniform symbolize his civilized war paint. From the officer's point of view, Ralph is hardly the prey of a deadly tribe but a boy who "needed a bath, a haircut, a nose-wipe, and a good deal of ointment." When he sees Jack's tribe wearing war paint and carrying spears, he assesses the situation as "Fun and games." Although he doesn't recognize it or understand his complicity in his own "fun and games," the naval officer has correctly identified the hunt: It's the sort of fun the Lord of the Flies assured Simon would take place on the island; the type of fun that, even at the time of the boys' rescue, is taking place on a larger scale with the war.

Theme

The officer echoes a sentiment expressed by Jack in Chapter 2 ("we're not savages. We're English . . . So we've got to do the right things"). Learning of the two deaths, the officer comments "I should have thought that a pack of British boys . . . would have . . . put up a better show than that." Both Jack and the officer are equally ignorant of the truth of the matter: Like all of humanity, these boys have and act on impulses that are at best uncivil and at worst deadly. In the novel, Golding uses events and mores associated with the British (his own culture), but his theme is universal. Although one could limit the interpretation to British imperialism (bestial aspects of British colonialism contrast sharply with the supremely polite British identity, for example), to do so would be to deny the larger truth: That all people—and therefore all societies—possess and display, to varying degrees, these deadly impulses.

Glossary

pax peace, here meant as a call for a truce.

acrid sharp, bitter, stinging, or irritating to the taste or smell.

inimical hostile; unfriendly.

gibber to speak or utter rapidly and incoherently; chatter unintelligibly.

essay to try; attempt.

antiphonal sung or chanted in alternation.

ululate to howl, hoot, or wail.

cordon a line or circle, as of soldiers or ships, stationed around an area to guard it.

diddle [Informal] to move back and forth jerkily or rapidly; juggle.

mold here, loose, soft, easily worked soil.

white drill a coarse linen or cotton cloth with a diagonal weave, used for work clothes, uniforms, etc.

epaulette shoulder ornament as for military uniforms.

cutter a boat carried, esp. formerly, aboard large ships to transport personnel or supplies.

rating an enlisted man in the Navy.

stern sheets the space at the stern of an open boat.

CHARACTER ANALYSES

The following character analyses delve into the physical, emotional, and psychological traits of the literary work's major characters so that you might better understand what motivates these characters. The writer of this study guide provides this scholarship as an educational tool by which you may compare your own interpretations of the characters. Before reading the character analyses that follow, consider first writing your own short essays on the characters as an exercise by which you can test your understanding of the original literary work. Then, compare your essays to those that follow, noting discrepancies between the two. If your essays appear lacking, that might indicate that you need to re-read the original literary work or re-familiarize yourself with the major characters.

Ralph

Ralph represents leadership, the properly socialized and civilized young man. He is attractive, charismatic, and decently intelligent. He demonstrates obvious common sense. Ralph is the one who conceives the meeting place, the fire, and the huts. He synthesizes and applies Piggy's intellectualism, and he recognizes the false fears and superstitions as barriers to their survival. He is a diplomat and a natural leader.

Ralph's capacity for leadership is evident from the very beginning (he is the only elected leader of the boys). During the crisis caused by the sight of the dead paratrooper on the mountain, Ralph is able to proceed with both sense and caution. He works vigilantly to keep the group's focus on the hope for rescue. When the time comes to investigate the castle rock, Ralph takes the lead alone, despite his fear of the so-called beast. Even in this tense moment, politeness is his default. When Simon mumbles that he doesn't believe in the beast, Ralph "answered him politely, as if agreeing about the weather." British culture is famed for civilized reserve in emotional times. By the standards of the society he's left behind, Ralph is a gentleman.

Having started with a schoolboy's romantic attitude toward anticipated "adventures" on the island, Ralph eventually loses his excitement about their independence and longs for the comfort of the familiar. He indulges in images of home, recollections of the peaceful life of cereal and cream and children's books he had once known. He fantasizes about bathing and grooming. Ralph's earlier life had been civilized, and he brought to the island innocent expectations and confidence until certain experiences informed his naiveté and destroyed his innocence. As he gains experience with the assemblies, the forum for civilized discourse, he loses faith in them. "Don't we love meetings?" Ralph says bitterly, frustrated that only a few of the boys actually follow through on their plans.

Over time, Ralph starts to lose his power of organized thought, such as when he struggles to develop an agenda for the meeting but finds himself lost in an inarticulate maze of vague thoughts. Ralph's loss of verbal ability bodes ill for the group because his authority lies in the platform, the symbol of collective governance and problem solving where verbal communication is the primary tool. Ralph's mental workings are subject to the same decay as his clothing; both are frayed by the rigors of the primitive life. Yet in response to the crisis of the lost rescue opportunity, Ralph demonstrates his capacities as a conceptual thinker.

When "[w]ith a convulsion of the mind, Ralph discovered dirt and decay," he is symbolically discovering humankind's dark side. At the same time, he has learned that intellect, reason, sensitivity, and empathy are the tools for holding the evil at bay. Ralph's awareness is evident when, realizing the difficulty of this lifestyle in contrast to his initial impression of its glamour, he "smiled jeeringly," as an adult might look back with cynicism on the ideals held as a youth.

Although he becomes worn down by the hardships and fears of primitive life and is gradually infected by the savagery of the other boys, Ralph is the only character who identifies Simon's death as murder and has a realistic, unvarnished view of his participation. He feels both loathing and excitement over the kill he witnessed. Once Ralph becomes prey, he realizes that he is an outcast "Cos I had some sense"—not just common sense but a sense of his identity as a civilized person, a sense of the particular morality that had governed the boys' culture back home. When Ralph encounters the officer on the beach at the end of the book, he is not relieved at being rescued from a certain grisly death but discomforted over "his filthy appearance," an indication that his civility had endured his ordeal. In exchange for his innocence, he has gained an understanding of humankind's natural character, an understanding not heretofore available to him: that evil is universally present in all people and requires a constant resistance by the intellect that was Piggy, by the mysticism and spiritualism that was Simon, and by the hopes and dreams that are his.

Jack

Jack represents evil and violence, the dark side of human nature. A former choirmaster and "head boy" at his school, he arrived on the island having experienced some success in exerting control over others by dominating the choir with his militaristic attitude. He is eager to make rules and punish those who break them, although he consistently breaks them himself when he needs to further his own interests. His main interest is hunting, an endeavor that begins with the desire for meat and builds to the overwhelming urge to master and kill other living creatures. Hunting develops the savagery that already ran close to his surface, making him "ape-like" as he prowls through the jungle. His domain is the emotions, which rule and fuel his animal nature.

The conflict on the island begins with Jack attempting to dominate the group rather than working with Ralph to benefit it. He frequently impugns the power of the conch, declaring that the conch rule does not matter on certain parts of the island. Yet he uses the conch to his advantage when possible, such as when he calls his own assembly to impeach Ralph. For him, the conch represents the rules and boundaries that have kept him from acting on the impulses to dominate others. Their entire lives in the other world, the boys had been moderated by rules set by society against physical aggression. On the island, however, that social conditioning fades rapidly from Jack's character. He quickly loses interest in that world of politeness and boundaries, which is why he feels no compunction to keep the fire going or attend to any of the other responsibilities for the betterment or survival of the group.

The dictator in Jack becomes dominant in his personality during the panic over the beast sighting on the mountain. In trying to get Ralph impeached, he uses his rhetorical skills to twist Ralph's words. In defense, he offers to the group a rationale that "He'd never have got us meat," asserting that hunting skills make for an effective leader. Jack assigns a high value only to those who he finds useful or agreeable to his views and looks to silence those who do not please him. Denouncing the rules of order, Jack declares, "We don't need the conch any more. We know who ought to say things." He dictates to his hunters that they forget the beast and that they stop having nightmares.

As Jack strives to establish his leadership, he takes on the title of "chief" and reinforces the illusion of station and power by using the other boys ceremoniously as standard bearers who raise their spears together and announce "The Chief has spoken." This role is no game for him, though; by the night of Simon's death, Jack has clearly gone power-mad, sitting at the pig roast on a large log "painted and garlanded . . . like an idol" while "[p]ower . . . chattered in his ear like an ape." His tribe addresses him as "Chief," indicating a form of more primitive tribal leadership.

True to Piggy's assertion that "It's them that haven't no common sense that make trouble on this island," Jack takes an entirely different direction from logic or common sense. Perhaps acting out of some guilt he is unable to acknowledge, Jack becomes paranoid and begins feeding misinformation to his tribe, a typical practice of dictatorships to control the collective thinking by controlling the information that is disseminated.

Given the thrill of "irresponsible authority" he's experienced on the island, Jack's return to civilization is conflicted. When the naval officer asks who is in charge, Jack starts to step forward to challenge Ralph's claim of leadership but is stopped perhaps by the recognition that now the old rules will be enforced.

Piggy

Piggy is the intellectual with poor eyesight, a weight problem, and asthma. He is the most physically vulnerable of all the boys, despite his greater intelligence. Piggy represents the rational world. By frequently quoting his aunt, he also provides the only female voice.

Piggy's intellect benefits the group only through Ralph; he acts as Ralph's advisor. He cannot be the leader himself because he lacks leadership qualities and has no rapport with the other boys. Piggy also relies too heavily on the power of social convention. He believes that holding the conch gives him the right to be heard. He believes that upholding social conventions get results.

As the brainy representative of civilization, Piggy asserts that "Life . . . is scientific." Ever the pragmatist, Piggy complains, "What good're your doing talking like that?" when Ralph brings up the highly charged issue of Simon's death at their hands. Piggy tries to keep life scientific despite the incident, "searching for a formula" to explain the death. He asserts that the assault on Simon was justifiable because Simon asked for it by inexplicably crawling out of the forest into the ring.

Piggy is so intent on preserving some remnant of civilization on the island that he assumes improbably enough that Jack's raiders have attacked Ralph's group so that they can get the conch when of course they have come for fire. Even up to the moment of his death, Piggy's perspective does not shift in response to the reality of their situation. He can't think as others think or value what they value. Because his eminently intellectual approach to life is modeled on the attitudes and rules of the authoritative adult world, he thinks everyone should share his values and attitudes as a matter of course. Speaking of the deaths of Simon and the littlun with the birthmark, he asks "What's grownups goin' to think?" as if he is not so much mourning the boys' deaths as he is mourning the loss of values, ethics, discipline, and decorum that caused those deaths.

Simon

Simon's role as an artistic, religious visionary is established not only by his hidden place of meditation but also by the description of his eyes: "so bright they had deceived Ralph into thinking him delightfully gay and wicked." While Piggy has the glasses—one symbol of vision and truth—Simon has bright eyes, a symbol of another kind of vision and truth.

Simon is different from the other boys not only due to his physical frailty, manifested in his fainting spells, but also in his consistently expressed concern for the more vulnerable boys. Littluns follow him, and he picks choice fruit for them from spots they can't reach, a saintly or Christ-like image. He stands up for Piggy and helps him get his glasses back when Jack knocks them off his head, another allusion to Simon's visionary bent. In addition, he has a secret place in the jungle, where he spends time alone.

Simon's loner tendencies make the other boys think he's odd, but, for the reader, Simon's credibility as a mystic is established when he prophesies to Ralph "You'll get back to where you came from." Simon reaches an abstract understanding of mankind's latent evil nature and unthinking urge to dominate as "mankind's essential illness." When Simon tries to visualize what the beast might look like, "there arose before his inward sight the picture of a human at once heroic and sick"—Golding's vision of humanity as flawed by inherent depravity. Golding gives this knowledge to an outsider like Simon to reflect the place visionaries or mystics typically hold in society: on the fringes, little understood by the majority, and often feared or disregarded. Like other mystics, Simon asks questions the other boys cannot answer. His questions to them, "What's the dirtiest thing there is?" and "What else is there to do?" require both abstract thought and courageous action to answer.

In contrast to Piggy and Ralph's equating adulthood with knowledge and higher understanding, Simon sees the darker side of knowledge. For him, the staked sow's eyes are "dim with the infinite cynicism of adult life," a view of adults not defined by the civilized politeness and capability the boys imagine. Yet Simon soldiers on in his quest to discover the identity of the beast on the mountaintop because he sees the need for the boys to face their fears, to understand the true identity of the false beast on the mountain, and to get on with the business of facing the beast within themselves.

By courageously seeking to confront the figure on the mountain-top, Simon fulfills his destiny of revelation. He doesn't get to share his revelation with the other boys because they are not ready to accept or understand it. Instead he dies as a result of being made the scapegoat for the boys' unshakeable fear. When Simon's body is carried off by the tide, covered in the jellyfish-like phosphorescent creatures who have come in with the tide, Golding shifts the focus from Simon's body's movements to the much larger progressions of the sun, moon, and earth because Simon represented a knowledge as fundamental as the elements.

Samneric

Samneric (Sam and Eric) represent totally civilized and socialized persons. As identical twins, they have always been a group, albeit the smallest of groups, but a group nevertheless. They know no other way than to submit to the collective identity and will. They are initially devoted to rescue but easily overwhelmed by the ferocity of tribe. They represent the well-intentioned members of general public who play by the rules of whoever is in charge. They are easily intimidated by Jack and abandon their fire-tending duties at his command. Seeing Ralph's rage at the resultant loss of a rescue opportunity, Samneric mock him once they are alone, despite the fact that their desertion of duty caused his anger and the loss of possible rescue. On a realistic, perhaps human, level, they may laugh to dispel their guilt or because their childish perspective has already allowed them to forget the loss they caused or because their priority is merely to avoid punishment. On the symbolic level, however, laughter is a totally social act.

After the horror of Simon's death, in which they participate, they fear for their own lives because they have remained loyal to Ralph. As Ralph's group plans to approach Jack's tribe, Samneric want to paint themselves like tribe members, hoping for mercy through assimilation. When the twins are captured by the tribe, Samneric "protested out of the heart of civilization" but abandon their loyalty to that civilization to avoid punishment, betraying Ralph out of concern for their own welfare. Their return to civilization will be fairly easy because they look only to appease whoever is in charge.

Roger

Roger represents the sadist, the individual who enjoys hurting others. His evil motives are different from Jack's, who pursues leadership and stature and enjoys the thrill of the hunt. Roger just likes to hurt people. He is described in Chapter 1 as a boy "who kept to himself with avoidance and secrecy." His secret is that he is, in some ways, more evil than even Jack. All his life, Roger has been conditioned to leash or mask his impulses. The "irresponsible authority" of Jack's reign offers him the chance to unleash his innate cruelty. Initially, in a mean-spirited prank, Roger throws rocks at the unsuspecting littlun, Henry, but he throws them *so that they miss*, surrounded as Henry is by "the protection of parents and school and policeman and the law. Roger's arm was conditioned by . . . civilization." Once he joins Jack's tribe, he has lost that conditioning and eventually kills Piggy with one boulder, which was not intended to miss.

Roger carves out a distinct niche in the tribe as the hangman, the torturer who plays a key role in all dictatorships, and relishes the role of a killer. From his point of view on top of Castle Rock, "Ralph was a shock of hair and Piggy a bag of fat"—not other human beings. Mentally dehumanizing those not in his group frees Roger from the restraints of decency, an effect he feels as "a sense of delirious abandonment" when he releases the rock to kill Piggy.

CRITICAL ESSAYS

On the pages that follow, the writer of this study guide provides critical scholarship on various aspects of Golding's *Lord of the Flies*. These interpretive essays are intended solely to enhance your understanding of the original literary work; they are supplemental materials and are not to replace your reading of *Lord of the Flies*. When you're finished reading *Lord of the Flies*, and prior to your reading this study guide's critical essays, consider making a bulleted list of what you think are the most important themes and symbols. Write a short paragraph under each bullet explaining why you think that theme or symbol is important; include at least one short quote from the original literary work that supports your contention. Then, test your list and reasons against those found in the following essays. Do you include themes and symbols that the study guide author doesn't? If so, this self test might indicate that you are well on your way to understanding original literary work. But if not, perhaps you will need to re-read *Lord of the Flies*.

Major Themes in the Novel

Lord of the Flies was driven by Golding's consideration of human evil, a complex topic that involves an examination not only of human nature but also the causes, effects, and manifestations of evil. It demands also a close observation of the methods or ideologies humankind uses to combat evil and whether those methods are effective. Golding addresses these topics through the intricate allegory of his novel.

The Problem of Evil

When *Lord of the Flies* was first released in 1954, Golding described the novel's theme in a publicity questionnaire as "an attempt to trace the defects of society back to the defects of human nature." In his 1982 essay *A Moving Target*, he stated simply "The theme of *Lord of the Flies* is grief, sheer grief, grief, grief." The novel ends of course with Ralph grieving the indelible mark of evil in each person's heart, an evil he scarcely suspected existed before witnessing its effects on his friends and supporters. The former schoolboys sought unthinkingly to dominate others who were not of their group. They discovered within themselves the urge to inflict pain and enjoyed the accompanying rush of power. When confronted with a choice between reason's civilizing influence and animality's self-indulgent savagery, they choose to abandon the values of the civilization that Ralph represents.

This same choice is made constantly all over the world, all throughout history—the source of the grief Golding sought to convey. He places supposedly innocent schoolboys in the protected environment of an uninhabited tropical island to illustrate the point that savagery is not confined to certain people in particular environments but exists in everyone as a stain on, if not a dominator of, the nobler side of human nature. Golding depicts the smallest boys acting out, in innocence, the same cruel desire for mastery shown by Jack and his tribe while hunting pigs and, later, Ralph. The adults waging the war that marooned the boys on the island are also enacting the desire to rule others.

Ironically, by giving rein to their urge to dominate, the boys find themselves in the grip of a force they can neither understand nor acknowledge. The Lord of the Flies tells Simon "Fancy thinking the Beast was something you could hunt and kill!" and then laughs at the boys' efforts to externalize their savagery in the form of an animal or other fearsome creature. Simon has the revelation that evil isn't simply a component of human nature, but an active element that seeks expression.

Contemporary Outlets for Violence

Most societies set up mechanisms to channel aggressive impulses into productive enterprises or projects. On the island, Jack's hunters are successful in providing meat for the group because they tap into their innate ability to commit violence. To the extent that this violence is a reasoned response to the group's needs (for example, to feed for the population), it produces positive effects and outcomes. However, when the violence becomes the motivator and the desired outcome lacks social or moral value beyond itself, as it does with the hunters, at that point the violence becomes evil, savage, and diabolical.

Violence continues to exist in modern society and is institutionalized in the military and politics. Golding develops this theme by having his characters establish a democratic assembly, which is greatly affected by the verbal violence of Jack's power-plays, and an army of hunters, which ultimately forms a small military dictatorship. The boys' assemblies are likened to both ends of the social or civil spectrum, from pre-verbal tribe gatherings to modern governmental institutions, indicating that while the forum for politics has changed over the millennia, the dynamic remains the same. Consider the emotional basis of the boys' choice of leaders: Initially they vote for Ralph not because he has demonstrated leadership skills but because of his charisma and arbitrary possession of the conch. Later they desert him—and the reasoned democracy he promotes—to join Jack's tribe because Jack's way of life, with the war paint and ritualized dance, seems like more fun. Choosing Jack's "fun" tribe indicates a dangerous level of emotionally based self-indulgence. By relying on emotion to decide the island's political format, the boys open themselves up to the possibility of violence because violence lies in the domain of emotion.

Yet Jack's mentality on a larger scale is not fun and games but warfare, a concept made clear at the end: When Ralph encounters the officer on the beach, he notices first not the officer's face but his uniform and revolver, which are the markings of the officer's tribe. The decorative elements of his uniform symbolize his war paint. His ship will be enacting the same sort of manhunt for his enemy that Jack's tribe conducts for Ralph.

The Effect of Fear

Golding addresses the effects of fear on the individual and on a group. For individuals, fear distorts reality such as when Samneric's terror at spotting the dead paratrooper magnifies their experience from merely seeing movement and hearing the parachute to being actively chased down the mountain as they flee. When the other boys hear Samneric's tale, the group dynamic of fear comes into play. The boys do not band together to overcome this fearful situation through unity but allow their own worst impulses to surface and dominate, fragmenting into opposing groups and killing one of their own in a frenzy of fear and savagery.

Speech and Silence

Golding gives a more subtle treatment to the theme concerning speech's role in civilization. He repeatedly represents verbal communication as the sole property of civilization while savagery is non-verbal, or silent. Despite the animal noises in the jungle, as an entity, the jungle emanates a silence even the hunter Jack finds intimidating. In fact all the boys find silence threatening; they become agitated when a speaker holding the conch in assembly falls silent.

The conch plays a key role in this theme because it symbolizes not only to the power *to* speak during assembly but also the power *of* speech, an ability that separates humans from animals. Following the death of Piggy and destruction of the conch, "the silence was complete" as if Piggy provided the last bastion of human intellect—or humanity itself—on the island.

Verbal communication is crucial to the development of abstract thought. "If only one had time to think!" Ralph laments. Civilization provides institutions where the individuals can devote themselves to mental activities. Simon created such a place in his hidden spot in the jungle. He found silence necessary to contemplate his vision of the beast. He was the only boy to understand the true identity of the much-feared beast and the only boy to whom the Lord of the Flies speaks. To bring about that conversation, the sow's head had to break the ultimate silence of death. Golding may depict silence as tremendously threatening because death does signify absolute silence, and the end of all hope.

While the conch's symbolic power remained alive to the boys, there was hope that they could continue with their small society peacefully and productively. With the loss of regulated discourse came the end of Ralph's humane influence on the boys.

Concept, Identity, and Manifestations of the Beast

Golding uses the boys' fear of a mythical beast to illustrate their assumption that evil arises from external forces rather than from themselves. This fearsome beast initially takes form in their imaginations as a snake-type animal that disguises itself as jungle vines; later, they consider the possibility of a creature that rises from the sea or the more nebulous entity of a ghost. When they spot the dead paratrooper who has landed on the mountain, the boys feel sure that they have proof of a beast's existence. In fact a beast does roam the island, but not in the form the boys imagine.

Concept

Golding wanted to illustrate in this novel the dark side of human nature and make the point that each member of humankind has this dark side. The boys conceptualize the source of all their worst impulses as a beast, some sort of actual animal or possibly supernatural creature inhabiting the island. Yet all along the boys take on the persona of the beast when they act on their animal impulses. There is no external beast.

Identity

Golding conveys the beast's identity through the literal actions of Jack and his tribe and through the abstract concept conveyed in Simon's vision. Simon's revelation about the beast comes upon him after he witnesses the sow's death and beheading. As an observer instead of a participant, Simon is able to comprehend the brutality of the act. The sow's head becomes covered with flies, creatures that lack the capacity to feel compassion for or empathy with the dead sow, occupied entirely by their need to eat and multiply. That compassion is one of the key dividers between humanity and animality; tellingly, Jack lacks compassion for the littluns and the vulnerable Piggy. Soon his hunters lose their compassion as well, seeking only to hunt meat and increase the numbers of their tribe or kill those who will not join.

When Simon hallucinates that the staked head is speaking to him, his perception of the other boys as the island's true threat is confirmed. The Lord of the Flies confirms that "You knew, didn't you? I'm part of you? Close, close, close! I'm the reason why it's no go? Why things are what they are?"

Note that the literal translation of the Greek word Beelzebub, a term used for the Judeo-Christian idea of Satan, is "lord of the flies," and flies feast on dead animals and excrement. When Simon asks the assembly "What's the dirtiest thing there is?" he looks for the answer "evil" but also included in that answer is decay and death. Ironically, Jack's excretory answer is partially correct.

Jack provides more insight into the beast's identity when he asserts that "The beast is a hunter," unwittingly implicating himself as part of the problem, a source of the boys' fears. His lust for power and authority causes him to commit and encourage savage acts against his own kind—an accurate measure of his depravity. Sitting in front of his tribe, "Power . . . chattered in his ear like an ape." The figurative devil on his shoulder is his own animality, looking to master other creatures.

Golding pairs the devolution of Jack's character with Simon's hallucinatory revelation to paint a complete picture of humankind's dark side—that which the boys call "the beast."

Manifestations

Part of Golding's intent was to demonstrate that the evil is not restricted to specific populations or situations. On the island, the beast is manifest in the deadly tribal dances, war paint, and the manhunt; in the outside world that same lust for power and control plays out as a nuclear war. Prior to the war, some of the boys, such as the perpetually victimized Piggy, experienced the brutality of others on the playground, an environment often idealized as the joyous site of a carefree childhood. Within civilized society the beast expresses itself in various ways: through acceptable venues such as the military; in unacceptable forms such as madness or criminality, which carries punitive repercussions; or concealed in the maneuvers of politics and other nonviolent power plays. In *Lord of the Flies* Golding illustrates that evil is present in everyone and everywhere; humankind's work lies not in the impossible mission of eradicating it but in the struggle to keep it from becoming the dominant force in our lives.

Golding's Use of the Fable Structure

A fable is a short fictional story intended to teach a moral lesson. Best known are Aesop's fables, which feature talking animals as the main characters and end with such truisms as "slow and steady wins the race." The one-dimensional characters and simplistic story line of a fable leave little room for argument with the concluding proverb. It is ironic, then, that Golding considered *Lord of the Flies* a fable, because his novel allows much room for speculation.

Instead of using cartoonish talking animals, Golding teaches his lesson with fully developed human characters representing the dominant motifs. As the characters interact with each other and with their environment, so do the forces they represent. Using the characters to embody these forces allows Golding the opportunity to compare and contrast with rich shadings of meaning rather than with simplistic oppositions. Unlike Aesop's animals, human beings act in ways that frequently conflict with the values they consciously hold, as is the case with Golding's protagonist Ralph. Because Ralph finds himself participating in the same savage behavior he condemns in the other boys, he presents a realistic picture of a humane person resorting to brutality under unusual circumstances.

Other characters also bring ambiguity to the motifs they embody. Piggy, for example, represents the scientific rationalist whose knowledge and intellect far exceed that of the other boys. Yet for all his intelligence, he cannot figure out how to speak so that the others will listen.

Golding does seek to provide a lesson in morality, but the lesson lacks the straightforward and decisive tone of the proverb that concludes most fables. At the end of Golding's fable, the reader has learned not that evil is confined to the militaristic portion of the population as epitomized by Jack; the pacifist Ralph participated in some of the brutal tribal activities. Neither has the reader learned that science or even simple common sense will save humanity from itself; Piggy is ridiculed throughout and then killed. Mystical revelations or visionary insight into the human condition will not save us; consider the fate of the saintly Simon. Instead the reader learns that evil lives in us all, and there is no proverb to remedy that situation. By invoking the complexity that underlies human nature, Golding's tale brings depth to the fable structure and presents a complex moral lesson as well.

CliffsNotes Review

Use this CliffsNotes Review to test your understanding of the original text and reinforce what you've learned in this book. After you work through the review and essay questions, identify the quote section, and the fun and useful practice projects, you're well on your way to understanding a comprehensive and meaningful interpretation of Golding's *Lord of the Flies*.

Q&A

1. What does the conch symbolize?

a. Jack's desire to hunt freely

b. eventual return to England

c. civilized discourse

2. When Roger sharpens a stick at both ends in preparation for Ralph's capture, what is it for?

3. What do Piggy's glasses symbolize?

a. intellectualism

b. success at building shelters

c. mystical visions

4. What was the sow doing when Jack and his hunters attacked her?

Answers: (1) c. (2) To impale Ralph's head as the savages did with the sow's. (3) a. (4) Nursing her piglets.

Identify the Quote: Find Each Quote in Lord of the Flies

1. Fancy thinking the Beast was something you could hunt and kill! You knew, didn't you? I'm part of you? Close, close, close! I'm the reason why it's no go? Why things are what they are?

2. This is our island. It's a good island. Until the grown-ups come to fetch us we'll have fun.

3. I agree with Ralph. We've got to have rules and obey them. After all, we're not savages . . . we've got to do the right things.

4. Things are breaking up. I don't understand why. We began well; we were happy . . . Then people started getting frightened.

5. What I mean is . . . maybe it's [the beast] only us.

6. You'll get back to where you came from.

Answers: (1) [Lord of the Flies, confirming Simon's suspicions that the beast exists in the boys' hearts, not in the jungle.] (2) [Ralph, telling the assembly on the first day his expectations for their island experience.] (3) [Jack, giving the assembly on the first day his own expectations for the group.] (4) [Ralph, opening for discussion at the assembly the issue of their nightmares and fears.] (5) [Simon, addressing the assembly during the discussion about the beast's possible identities and revealing his insightful nature.] (6) [Simon, prophesying to Ralph his eventual return.]

Essay Questions

1. In Chapter 5, Golding writes, "In a moment the platform was full of arguing, gesticulating shadows. To Ralph, seated, this seemed the breaking up of sanity." How is sanity defined? How does this novel contribute to an understanding of sanity and of madness? What are some other instances of madness in the novel?

2. Explain Piggy's point of view when he responds, "Course there aren't [ghosts] . . . 'Cos things wouldn't make sense. Houses an' streets, an'—TV—they wouldn't work" (Chapter 5). What does Piggy mean when he says that technology couldn't function if a supernatural beings existed?

3. Ralph says in Chapter 12 "there was that indefinable connection between himself and Jack; who therefore would never let him alone; never." What is that connection? How does it develop and what does it signify?

4. When Simon sees the Lord of the Flies, Golding writes that his "gaze was held by that ancient inescapable recognition" (Chapter 8). What recognition is Golding referring to?

5. Why does Simon's role as a visionary make him an outcast in the group? What other visionaries have been outcasts in their societies?

6. How does Golding use color to link Jack with the Lord of the Flies? Are there other instances of Golding using color to link characters or provide symbolism?

7. In Chapter 11, when Ralph announces that he's calling an assembly, he is greeted with silence. How do silence and speech function in this novel, and why is silence so threatening to the boys?

8. In Chapter 3, Piggy asks the boys "How can you expect to be rescued if you don't put first things first and act proper?" What does Piggy mean by "act proper?" Why does he feel acting properly will bring them success in being rescued? Contrast this sentiment to the actual reason a rescue ship spots their smoke signal.

9. Who or what is being described with this phrase: "There was the brilliant world of hunting, tactics, fierce exhilaration, skill, and there was the world of longing and baffled common-sense" (Chapter 4)? How do the two worlds represent facets of humanity?

10. Describe some of the ways the vision of a human "at once heroic and sick" (Chapter 6) is represented in the novel and within the larger context of history as well. Does Golding prescribe a remedy for the "sickness"?

Practice Projects

1. Create a Web site to introduce *Lord of the Flies* to other readers. Design pages to intrigue and inform your audience, and invite other readers to post their thoughts and responses to their reading of the novel. Check out other student-constructed sites for ideas, such as http://www.per-net.net/~chadly1/lord_of_the_flies/index.html   or http://webboards.virtualave.net/flies/.

2. Develop a screenplay for a film version of the book. Indicate which scenes you'd depict, which actors you'd like to cast, what special effects you'd use for Simon's encounter with the Lord of the Flies, and so on.

3. Write a brief skit showing the novel's essential events playing out in a different environment, such on an American farm, in the center of London, or on the streets of Paris.

CliffsNotes Resource Center

The learning doesn't need to stop here. CliffsNotes Resource Center shows you the best of the best—links to the best information in print and online about the author and/or related works. And don't think that this is all we've prepared for you; we've put all kinds of pertinent information at www.cliffsnotes.com. Look for all the terrific resources at your favorite bookstore or local library and on the Internet. When you're online, make your first stop www.cliffsnotes.com where you'll find more incredibly useful information about *Lord of the Flies*.

Books

This CliffsNotes book provides a meaningful interpretation of *Lord of the Flies,* published by Wiley Publishing, Inc. If you are looking for information about the author and/or related works, check out these other publications:

> *Critical Essays on William Golding,* edited by James R. Baker, is a useful collection of essays chosen by an expert on Golding. It addresses Golding's work through *The Paper Men* and includes transcripts of Golding's 1983 Nobel Lecture; it also includes as a brief interview. Boston: G.K. Hall & Co., 1988.

> *William Golding,* by Lawrence S. Friedman, is a comprehensive work that clearly explicates Golding's full body of fiction and provides an eloquent depiction of his achievements and the influences in his personal background. New York: Continuum Publishing, 1993.

> *William Golding,* by James Gindin. A slim volume addressing Golding's novels up through *The Paper Men*, it covers underlying themes and influences common to all of his fiction as well as analyses of individual novels. New York: St. Martin's Press, 1988.

> *William Golding: A Critical Study,* by Mark Kinkead-Weekes and Ian Gregor. Considered by many to be an ideal introduction to Golding's novels for its accessible yet detailed readings, this work addresses novels up through *Rites of Passage*. London: Faber and Faber, 1984.

> *William Golding,* by Kevin McCarron. A short but incredibly useful book that contains much information and insight in few pages, this book includes an annotated bibliography for further study. Plymouth, England: Northcote House, 1994.

It's easy to find books published by Wiley Publishing, Inc.. You'll find them in your favorite bookstores (on the Internet and at a store near you). We also have three Web sites that you can use to read about all the books we publish:

- www.cliffsnotes.com

- www.dummies.com

- www.wiley.com

Internet

Check out these Web resources for more information about William Golding and *Lord of the Flies*:

NovelGuide.com Home Page, http://www.novelguide.com/ lordoftheflies/—NovelGuide.com provides analyses of classic and contemporary literature. The site contains plot summaries, character profiles, metaphor and theme analyses, and key quotes as well as brief author biographies.

Homework-online.com Home Page, http://www.homework-online.com/homework-online/lotf/index.html— This site offers brief author biographies, key quotes, and material on theme, symbolism, character analysis, and chapter summaries. A unique feature is a hand-drawn map of the island.

Lord of the Flies Home Page, http://www.pernet.net/ ~chadly1/lord_of_the_flies/index.html—This graphics-intensive site is an incredible resource devoted to *Lord of the Flies*. The site provides links to other Internet resources, an introduction to Golding's body of work, a plot summary, in-depth character analyses, and sample essay questions with short answers.

Lord of the Flies Interactive Novel Study, http://webboards.virtualave.net/flies/—This award-winning site provides a plot summary, character and theme analyses, quizzes about the plot line, and an interactive bulletin board.

Lord of the Flies Info Page, http://www.gerenser.com/lotf/— Another award-winner, this site contains character analyses, chapter summaries and analyses, material on "analysis.html", a vocabulary section, links to other Web resources, and an interactive bulletin board.

Next time you're on the Internet, don't forget to drop by www.cliffsnotes.com. We created an online Resource Center that you can use today, tomorrow, and beyond.

Films

For film production of *Lord of the Flies*, see the following resources:

Lord of the Flies, Home Vision Cinema, 1963. Directed by Peter Brook, this black and white film was not very well received by critics, who felt the production was overblown and that the storyline was handled in too obvious a fashion. As with all movie adaptations of novels, some elements of the story have been changed. Most problematic is the film's exclusion of Simon's encounter with the Lord of the Flies.

Lord of the Flies, Columbia Pictures, 1990. Directed by Harry Hook, this color version of the book received even worse reviews than its predecessor. Not only does it leave out Simon's encounter with the Lord of the Flies, it also departs significantly from the novel in depiction of the characters and events. Rated R.

Send Us Your Favorite Tips

In your quest for knowledge, have you ever experienced that sublime moment when you figure out a trick that saves time or trouble? Perhaps you realized you were taking ten steps to accomplish something that could have taken two. Or you found a little-known workaround that achieved great results. If you've discovered a useful tip that gave you insight into or helped you understand *Lord of the Flies* and you'd like to share it, the CliffsNotes staff would love to hear from you. Go to our Web site at www.cliffsnotes.com and click the Talk to Us button. If we select your tip, we may publish it as part of CliffsNotes Daily, our exciting, free e-mail newsletter. To find out more or to subscribe to a newsletter, go to http://www.cliffs-notes.com on the Web.

INDEX

NOTES

NOTES

NOTES

_____
_____
_____
_____
_____
_____
_____
_____
_____
_____
_____
_____
_____
_____
_____
_____
_____
_____
_____
_____
_____
_____
_____
_____

CliffsNotes

LITERATURE NOTES

Absalom, Absalom!
The Aeneid
Agamemnon
Alice in Wonderland
All the King's Men
All the Pretty Horses
All Quiet on the
   Western Front
All's Well &
   Merry Wives
American Poets of the
   20th Century
American Tragedy
Animal Farm
Anna Karenina
Anthem
Antony and Cleopatra
Aristotle's Ethics
As I Lay Dying
The Assistant
As You Like It
Atlas Shrugged
Autobiography of
   Ben Franklin
Autobiography of
   Malcolm X
The Awakening
Babbit
Bartleby & Benito
   Cereno
The Bean Trees
The Bear
The Bell Jar
Beloved
Beowulf
The Bible
Billy Budd & Typee
Black Boy
Black Like Me
Bleak House
Bless Me, Ultima
The Bluest Eye & Sula
Brave New World
The Brothers Karamazov

The Call of the Wild &
   White Fang
Candide
The Canterbury Tales
Catch-22
Catcher in the Rye
The Chosen
The Color Purple
Comedy of Errors…
Connecticut Yankee
The Contender
The Count of
   Monte Cristo
Crime and Punishment
The Crucible
Cry, the Beloved
   Country
Cyrano de Bergerac
Daisy Miller &
   Turn…Screw
David Copperfield
Death of a Salesman
The Deerslayer
Diary of Anne Frank
Divine Comedy-I.
   Inferno
Divine Comedy-II.
   Purgatorio
Divine Comedy-III.
   Paradiso
Doctor Faustus
Dr. Jekyll and Mr. Hyde
Don Juan
Don Quixote
Dracula
Electra & Medea
Emerson's Essays
Emily Dickinson Poems
Emma
Ethan Frome
The Faerie Queene
Fahrenheit 451
Far from the Madding
   Crowd
A Farewell to Arms
Farewell to Manzanar
Fathers and Sons
Faulkner's Short Stories

Faust Pt. I & Pt. II
The Federalist
Flowers for Algernon
For Whom the Bell Tolls
The Fountainhead
Frankenstein
The French
   Lieutenant's Woman
The Giver
Glass Menagerie &
   Streetcar
Go Down, Moses
The Good Earth
The Grapes of Wrath
Great Expectations
The Great Gatsby
Greek Classics
Gulliver's Travels
Hamlet
The Handmaid's Tale
Hard Times
Heart of Darkness &
   Secret Sharer
Hemingway's
   Short Stories
Henry IV Part 1
Henry IV Part 2
Henry V
House Made of Dawn
The House of the
   Seven Gables
Huckleberry Finn
I Know Why the
   Caged Bird Sings
Ibsen's Plays I
Ibsen's Plays II
The Idiot
Idylls of the King
The Iliad
Incidents in the Life of
   a Slave Girl
Inherit the Wind
Invisible Man
Ivanhoe
Jane Eyre
Joseph Andrews
The Joy Luck Club
Jude the Obscure

Julius Caesar
The Jungle
Kafka's Short Stories
Keats & Shelley
The Killer Angels
King Lear
The Kitchen God's Wife
The Last of the
   Mohicans
Le Morte d'Arthur
Leaves of Grass
Les Miserables
A Lesson Before Dying
Light in August
The Light in the Forest
Lord Jim
Lord of the Flies
The Lord of the Rings
Lost Horizon
Lysistrata & Other
   Comedies
Macbeth
Madame Bovary
Main Street
The Mayor of
   Casterbridge
Measure for Measure
The Merchant
   of Venice
Middlemarch
A Midsummer Night's
   Dream
The Mill on the Floss
Moby-Dick
Moll Flanders
Mrs. Dalloway
Much Ado About
   Nothing
My Ántonia
Mythology
Narr. …Frederick
   Douglass
Native Son
New Testament
Night
1984
Notes from the
   Underground

CliffsNotes™
@ cliffsnotes.com

Check Out the All-New CliffsNotes Guides

TECHNOLOGY TOPICS

PERSONAL FINANCE TOPICS

CAREER TOPICS